POCKET GUIDE TO CHRISTIAN BELIEFS

I. HOWARD MARSHALL

InterVarsity Press
Downers Grove
Illinois 60515

Second American printing, February 1980,
by InterVarsity Press, with permission from Universities
and Colleges Christian Fellowship,
Leicester, England.

InterVarsity Press is the book-publishing division of
Inter-Varsity Christian Fellowship,
a student movement active on campus at hundreds
of universities, colleges and schools of nursing.
For information about local and regional
activities, write IVCF, 233 Langdon St.,
Madison, WI 53703.

Distributed in Canada through InterVarsity Press,
1875 Leslie St., Unit 10, Don Mills,
Ontario M3B 2M5, Canada.

ISBN 0-87784-504-2
Library of Congress Catalog Card Number: 78-2077

Printed in the United States of America

Preface

Every Christian ought to have a working knowledge of Christian doctrine. There are not many books, however, which attempt to give the basic essentials in short compass, so that the reader may obtain a reasonably complete bird's-eye view of the subject. The present book aims to do just that. It is intended to be the kind of simple, short, straightforward introduction to the subject which most young Christians find they need.

Although I have deliberately tried to be brief, I have at the same time attempted to cover all the main aspects of the Christian faith. Perhaps this method carries with it the danger that when a person has read this book he may think he knows it all. I hope that it will rather have the effect of encouraging readers to go further into the subject, perhaps by graduating to the fuller treatment by the late T. C. Hammond, *In understanding be men* (now available in a revised edition by D. F. Wright).

Not many readers will want to read this book through at a sitting. It is meant to be a study-book, and I hope that readers will take the time to turn up the various scriptural references which have been provided throughout the text. References to longer passages of Scripture have also been included for each major section. These have two purposes. First, it can be dangerous to base doctrine on isolated proof-texts without examining them in their contexts to determine their true meaning, and therefore it is good to consult, where possible, an extended passage dealing with the subject in question. Second, it is hoped that these passages, along with the questions provided at the end of each chapter, may provide a basis for group or individual Bible study on each aspect of Christian doctrine.

The present book is a revision of an earlier edition of the book, published in 1963. I have attempted to clarify the discussion throughout and to include fuller treatment of various issues. In its first edition the book has proved its usefulness in many ways. One minister used to give copies of it to couples whom he married. It has been a textbook in a class on Christian doctrine in a Bible College. I am grateful that so many people have found some help in it, and I pray that in this new form it may be of some use to Christians who want to have a better knowledge of their faith.

In the compilation of the first edition of this book Donald English played a notable part. To him and to all who have helped in any way in the production of this and the earlier edition I would like to express my warm thanks.

Howard Marshall

1

Why study Christian doctrine?

The first book of theology I ever studied boldly headed its first chapter with the title, *The queen of the sciences – Theology*, and the writer claimed: 'Seeing that Theology has for its domain the knowledge of God and His works, it is only just to regard it as the noblest of all the sciences – the very queen of the sciences'. Today we are not sure of its position, and one wag has said that it might be better called 'The knave of arts'. Within universities and colleges, Christian theology is often regarded as an unscientific subject using its own highly subjective methods and producing results which can have no possible claim to scientific validity. It has become fashionable to turn away from theology to 'religious studies', the comparative examination and description of the various religions of mankind, including Christianity, from an allegedly impartial and scientific point of view.

If the study of Christian theology is not highly regarded in Faculties of Arts, the individual Christian may well wonder whether it is worth his attention. If it is to be studied at all, let this be done by ministers and preachers who have a professional interest in it. The ordinary Christian does not need to burrow deeply into a subject which seems to have caused lots of confusion in the church and which has little apparent relevance to the Christian life. Is it not the case that on occasion people who have dabbled in theology have become bewildered in their faith and even 'unsound'? And have we not all heard of young people, keen in Christian service, who went away to theological college and emerged again after three or four years with all the life knocked out of them and their cherished beliefs reduced to a sad state of confusion? Beware, then, of reading any further in a book such as this one!

But of course all this is a sad caricature of the real position – although, admittedly, with sufficient grains of truth in it to make a reader wonder whether the author can possibly present a convincing case for taking up theology.

Many universities and colleges nowadays have departments devoted to the study of politics. One of the lecturers in the subject during my student days resigned his post to work in the headquarters of a political party. Clearly he had a particular commitment to the truth of one political outlook, and he was (and is) by no means alone in his allegiance. Another lecturer, whose own politics are probably somewhat pinkish in colour, told me that he keeps his own allegiance dark, so that the students will not think that they have got him nicely pigeon-holed and be able to say, 'He only says that because he is a . . .' Lecturers in politics and other subjects are very often committed to the truth of one understanding of the subject. Yet this does not prevent them from attempting to teach their subject objectively and scientifically, and in general people do not question their good faith. The situation of the theologian is somewhat similar. He is committed to the truth of what he teaches, and he knows that often other people do not share his beliefs; nevertheless, he aims to teach with academic integrity and impartiality, and he is prepared to question and examine his own beliefs so that they are well-founded.

There is clearly a difference between the study of theology and religious studies. The latter is largely descriptive and comparative and attempts to understand the various religions in terms of the natural causes and influences which account for their particular histories and characteristics. The former sets out the content of Christian belief, but does so in terms of its nature as a statement of what Christians *ought* to believe. It accepts the Christian faith as true, and attempts to state it systematically. Now, of course, there can also be Muslim theology or Buddhist theology, statements of what the adherents of these religions consider to be true, produced by people who believe in their truth. Fair enough. It is then possible to compare these systems and to see what elements of truth each of them may contain by comparison with one's own position and to discuss the basis on which each of them is constructed. Although the Christian will work from his Christian standpoint, he will nevertheless be open to consider what elements of truth there may be in these other systems.

There is a place, then, for both theological study and religious studies, and in both cases it is possible to work with intellectual honesty and with an open mind.

What is theology?

Before we ask what value there may be in the study of theology or Christian doctrine, it may be helpful to ask exactly what is involved in the study itself. 'Theology' is a word of a familiar type, being similar to words like 'biology', 'pharmacology', and so on, in which the '-*ology*' part designates the study or science of the subject denoted by the first half of the word; in this case '*theo*-' is derived from the Greek word *theos*, meaning God, and hence theology is the study of God. The other word in use, 'doctrine', is derived from a Latin word which means 'teaching', so that Christian doctrine is what Christians teach.

It follows from these considerations that the subject-matter of theology is God. Naturally it is not concerned merely with God in himself, but with the activity of God and with every area of human thought and experience which is affected by belief in God.

But we are talking about *Christian* theology, and therefore the concern of the theologian is with what Christians believe about God. Christian doctrine is *a statement of what Christians believe*. Such statements might be found in the creeds and confessions of the church which were drawn up to express the beliefs of those who framed them. The task of theology is to state what Christians believe in a systematic and orderly fashion.

We may look at the matter from another point of view. We have just been speaking about what Christians believe, as if Christian faith were a matter of believing certain things in our heads, statements that can be expressed in propositional form. But the simplest Christian knows that Christian faith is primarily a matter of trusting in God through Jesus Christ. Theology, therefore, asks the question, What does it mean to have a personal trust in God? We can say that theology is an expression of *what it means to trust in God*, and this way of putting the matter does justice to the fact that Christian belief is more than simply assenting to certain statements (which even demons can do, Jas. 2:19).

We might be tempted to think that Christian theology is thus based primarily on the introspection of believers as they ask themselves what it is that they believe – and there might be as many different theologies as there are believers. But the *source* of Christian theology is not primarily Christian experience, but rather divine revelation. Our knowledge of God depends on what God has revealed of himself to men, and our Christian experience itself is determined by this revelation, which tells us what is involved in belief in God. While God has revealed himself in many different ways, the primary revelation is to be found in the Bible. This records the historical events in which God was especially active to reveal himself, and, above all, presents the historical person of Jesus, through whom came his supreme revelation. It also gives the inspired 'commentary' by prophets and apostles, which brings out the significance of these events. This point will require fuller elucidation later, but for the moment we can say that Christian doctrine is *an exposition of God's revelation of himself in the Bible*.

There are, of course, other views of the source of Christian theology. Some people would attach much more importance to the analysis of the religious experience of Christians. Others would attempt to develop Christian theology on the basis of the revelation of God in nature or on the basis of philosophical discussion. Clearly there is a place for such studies within Christian doctrine, but the standpoint of this book is that the Bible is the basic and normative source for Christian doctrine, and that other sources of knowledge stand in a subordinate position to its supreme authority.

This consideration is based on the nature of the Bible as the principal and clearest place of God's self-revelation to men. In theology we are bound by what God has said and are not free to indulge our own speculations, which may be right or wrong. Christian theology, accordingly, has a normative or binding quality. It is not simply a descriptive statement of what Christians believe; it expresses what Christians *ought* to believe on the basis of God's revelation. This aspect of the subject is sometimes indicated by the use of the term 'dogmatics'.

Christian doctrine and Bible study

If we already have God's revelation in the Bible, someone may well ask why we need to study Christian doctrine: surely it is sufficient to be a Bible student without bothering about doctrine? Perhaps the simplest answer to this question is that anybody who studies the Bible is, in fact, really studying doctrine. When one of our universities instituted a 'Department of Biblical History and Literature', the hope of the founders may have been that the Bible would be studied without any reference to doctrine or theology. One might as well hope to study the works of Shakespeare without reference to their literary quality.

The Bible is a doctrinal book, and it cannot be studied with-

13

out some reference to that fact. But the Bible is not a systematic statement of doctrine. Paul, for example, did not set out to write systematic theological treatises when he wrote his epistles (with the possible exception of Romans); he was writing occasional documents, meant to deal with the current problems and needs of particular congregations. But his writings presuppose his understanding of Christian theology, and that understanding is expressed piecemeal in them. The theologian tries to work out from his epistles the systematic character of his thinking. Again, what the Bible has to say on any particular topic is not necessarily to be found all in one place. (That is why the most useful aid to Bible study after the Bible itself is a concordance.) The teaching of the Bible about creation is not confined to the first chapters of Genesis, but is spread through many passages such as Psalm 8, Isaiah 40 and Colossians 1. In order to understand what the Bible says on any topic, it is necessary to assemble all the relevant passages, compare them with one another and so arrive at a comprehensive statement of the teaching of the Bible.

And we cannot stop there. What the Bible says about creation needs to be related to the discoveries of scientists and the insights of philosophers, so that the Christian may have a critical understanding of the thinking of his contemporaries and may be able to frame his own understanding of creation, based on all available sources of knowledge and intelligible to modern people. Christian theology thus involves relating what the Bible teaches to men's knowledge gained in other ways. If all truth is God's truth, then the Christian cannot spurn any source of knowledge in attempting to find out how God has revealed himself. This applies even to the teaching of other religions and philosophical systems, which may contain a mixture of truth and error. To most Christians the teachings of Karl Marx appear to be diametrically opposed to Christian belief, but it would be foolish to ignore the possibility that somewhere in the Communist system of thinking there may be insights into human nature and behaviour which are true in themselves, independent of the non-Christian framework in which they appear.

A systematic discussion of Christian theology will take the student to many sources of knowledge and areas of thinking. Our purpose in the present book will be the more modest one of attempting to set out the biblical teaching which forms the foundation of Christian theology.

The use of the Bible in theology

How is the Bible to be used in the study of Christian doctrine? A few comments may not be out of place.

First, it must be emphasized that the Bible is the principal source for the theologian. It is here, as we shall see in the next chapter, that God has revealed himself to us most fully. Consequently all other sources of knowledge about God must be tested by the Bible.

Next, we need to study the message of the Bible as a whole and to interpret the various individual parts of it in their contexts. In the past, some theologians have been strongly and justifiably criticized because they based their theology on 'proof-texts' which they dragged indiscriminately from all parts of the Bible and whose interpretation they took for granted without asking what they really meant. Some of the curious views of the sects result from this procedure. A man once tried to use a verse in Ecclesiastes (I think it was 3:19f.) to prove to me that there is no after-life. He did not stop to ask what the text in question originally meant, nor to ask how it fitted in with the teaching of the New Testament, which clearly testifies to an after-life. It is always best to study whole passages rather than isolated texts and to 'compare Scripture with Scripture'.

A third point is that we should not despise the many helps to the study of the Bible that exist. Some people like to go it alone, thinking that their own insight into the Bible is sufficient, and that the Bible itself will be plain and transparent to their understanding. No doubt the main thrust of the Bible is clear enough, and the Reformers were right to insist on what they called the 'perspicuity' of Scripture, over against the mass of traditions which had obscured its meaning in the medieval church; but it would be sheer presumption on the part of any Christian to think that he can ignore the wisdom that God has given to other Christians and do his own thing successfully. There is a vast secondary literature in which the collective wisdom of God's people is to be found, and here there is light to be found on the dark places of the Bible. By careful use of such books, we can vastly increase our own understanding of Scripture.

It goes without saying that the student of theology needs the guidance of the Spirit to help him in his task. There can be no better aid than the help of the Author himself to understand his book. A willingness to learn humbly from the Spirit of God is indispensable to the theologian, lest he be led astray by the pride and self-sufficiency of a human mind that thinks that it has the native ability to understand the ways of God.

The uses of Christian doctrine

What is the ultimate value of this study, which Christians may be tempted to set aside as too difficult or simply as irrelevant to their Christian lives? As Paul said in answer to a different question, 'much in every way'. One obvious reply is that the study of Christian doctrine will preserve the student from falling into error and enable him to distinguish between what is true and false. A few years ago a number of people in a somewhat exclusive Christian sect, which up until then had managed to stay reasonably orthodox, were directed into some highly eccentric behaviour at the behest of a man who had attained a position of influence among them. It took a few years before many of them realized how they had been duped by a man whose teaching was crazy and whose own character fell far below Christian standards; it is safe to say that had the members of this group studied doctrine more seriously and tested the instructions given to them by Scripture, they would not have been led astray as they were. In the sixteenth century there were Christians who practised polygamy out of a mistaken understanding of Christian freedom, and today there are people who observe Saturday as their day of worship out of a confusion between the Jewish Sabbath and the Christian Lord's Day. The antidote to such oddities is a sound knowledge of Christian doctrine.

At a more serious and personal level, Christian doctrine feeds the soul of the believer and enables him to grow in Christian faith and understanding. Although the study of doctrine can be merely a matter of the mind, the mind can be the route by which the Word of God reaches the heart and influences the life. Christian doctrine, studied in a spirit of humility and prayer, opens up the mind to the revelation of God and provides spiritual food for the believer. He learns more of the character of the God whom he worships, he understands more fully the tragic situation from which he has been saved, he appreciates more fully the wonder of the divine grace which saved him, and he realizes more of the spiritual possessions which God wishes to bestow upon him.

Christian doctrine thus provides the fuel for devotion. It sets the heart on fire with love for God and gives the inspiration for worship. It is arguable that much Christian worship is cold and formal, simply because it lacks an adequate basis in the presentation of Christian doctrine. Christian worship is the human response to divine revelation, and it is only when worship is based on the presentation of the Word of God to the congregation that they can respond with warmed hearts and give God intelligent praise and service.

Finally, only through the study of doctrine can the Christian

prepare himself to be active in applying his faith to the problems of living and to the task of Christian witness. The evangel-
ist must know his message and understand how it applies to
the needs of the many different kinds of people whom he will
meet. A person who does not understand the gospel will be a
very poor advocate for it; he cannot expect to be persuasive if
he has not studied his brief.

With these practical applications in mind, we can now turn
to our subject. We shall look first in more detail at how we know
about God (ch. 2) and then at the nature of God (ch. 3) and of
the world, its creation and its fall into sin (ch. 4). This will lead
on to consideration of God's new start with the sinful world in
Jesus Christ (ch. 5), and how God's new creation becomes
effective in the individual (ch. 6) and the church (ch. 7). Finally,
we shall look at the completion of God's work at the end of
time (ch. 8).

Questions for study and discussion

1. *A Unitarian minister once put up a poster saying that he
offered 'religion without dogma'. Do you think that what he
offered is possible?*

2. *Can a Christian believer study religion or theology 'with an
open mind'?*

3. *Is it possible for a person who is not himself a Christian to
understand Christian doctrine fully?*

4. *It has been said that 'deep theology is the best fuel for devotion': discuss.*

5. *Many sects base their peculiar doctrines on the teaching of the
Bible. How would you show the validity or otherwise of their
views?*

18

2

Our knowledge of God

Christian doctrine tells us what Christians believe about God. But before we can discuss what we believe about God, we must tackle the preliminary question of how we come to know about God, and to learn about his existence, character and actions This question is one of crucial importance, for the differences between the various theological positions Christians hold very often depend on differences in how knowledge of God is thought to be obtained.

There is a popular Christian song which may suggest a possible answer to our question. The chorus of the song contains the rousing claim 'Christ Jesus lives today' and offers a statement of the resurrection of Jesus. The composer goes on to pose the question, 'You ask me how I know he lives?' and then answers himself: 'He lives within my heart'. How do you know and prove that Jesus Christ is alive today? The answer of this writer is that we can appeal to the experience of his presence in our hearts. From which it is a short step to the conclusion that by putting down our experience on paper we are recording Christian doctrine.

Years ago there was written a book entitled *The theology of experience*. Today it is virtually forgotten, but its title may serve as a summary of this kind of approach. It would stress that knowledge and certainty in religion come not from intellectual argument, but from inward conviction. There is an element of truth here. A person can know all about Christianity in his head through argument and reasoning, but unless he also knows it in his heart, then it will not make much difference to his living. His theology will remain cold and abstract, just as was the case with John Wesley, whose correct knowledge of the gospel remained dull and lifeless until the occasion when he felt his heart 'strangely warmed' and what he already knew in his head became a matter of personal experience and conviction. We cannot do without Christian experience.

Not surprisingly, then, some people have thought that writing Christian doctrine consists in setting down what your Christian experience has taught you. After all, the scientist does something like this. He does his experiments. By personal discovery he finds out what is going on, and he then formulates his results and offers an explanation of his experience. Science depends upon the experimental method. Should not theology proceed in the same way?

It sounds excellent, but it doesn't work. For it is very easy to confuse faith and feelings. A person's consciousness of the presence of God with him may vary from day to day, and seem different when circumstances change. Experience is a very shifting foundation in matters of religion. Then, again, a person might begin to compare his experience with that of other people, and discover that theirs was different from his own. They might not even explain their experience in terms of God at all. Even among Christians there are enormous differences in outlook and feelings. Sooner or later one would have to ask, How do I know which of my experiences to trust? How can I compare the experiences of different people and know which is right? These questions cannot be answered on the level of experience.

Perhaps, then, we should try something more objective and reliable. Suppose that for experience we were to substitute reason. For the use of reason can lead to much more certain knowledge, as in the case of mathematical reasoning. It is not surprising that this course has been tried in theology. In fact an element of reason must enter into theology. Even when we spoke of using experience as a foundation, it was implied that we must think about the significance of our experience, and to think is to reason. And to think about thinking about theology, as we are doing just now, is certainly to use our reason. Clearly we cannot do theology without employing reason, any more than we can leave emotion and experience out of religion.

But the suggestion goes further than this. It is that thinking and reasoning are the source of our knowledge of God and his ways. Philosophers, for example, have produced arguments for the existence of God, based on the use of reason, and have tried to deduce what he is like and how he acts. Theology has been regarded as a system of ideas which can be discovered by reason.

But once again we must be critical, and ask whether this approach really works. There are two main objections. Are our minds big enough to think properly about God? From our fairly simple knowledge of God as Christians we have reason to believe that he is infinite. How, then, can our minds possibly measure up to the task of understanding him? The thing is impossible. Again, even if we do manage to form a mental understanding of God, how do we know that it corresponds to reality? How do we know that our ideas correspond to what is real? How do we know by the use of reason that God is there?

The effect of arguments such as these is to suggest that reason should be conscious of its own limitations. Plainly reason isn't the key to theology, although, like experience, it has its value and cannot be set aside. What has gone wrong is that in both cases we have started with man, trying to discover by his own abilities what God is like and not getting on very well. What we need is some evidence of the activity of God, something that God does to make himself known to us, in other words, revelation. So far we have been talking about discovery by man; what we need is revelation by God. Of course the two go together; revelation must be discovered by man and received by the use of his faculties, but our difficulty has arisen because we began from the wrong end, and started with man instead of with God. Experience and reason must both have something to work on, or else they will remain empty. And the conclusions of both experience and reason must be capable of being tested by some external, objective standard, or else their conclusions will remain uncertain and ill-founded.

It is, therefore, fundamental to realize that, if there is a God, he can be known only through his own revelation of himself: 'Through God alone can God be known'. What we must now ask is whether and how God has revealed himself to human apprehension.

Revelation in nature (Isaiah 40)

In almost every age and culture men have been led to believe in some power or powers greater than themselves through considering the nature of the world around them (*cf*. Ps. 19:1). The very fact that there is a world at all has led men to ask whether it came into existence by itself or does not suggest the activity of a creator (the so-called *cosmological* argument for the existence of God). Again, the universe is not a haphazard concourse of parts, but shows evidence of structure and even of beauty: one may well ask whether the evidence of 'design' does not point to the existence of a designer (the *teleological* argument). Finally, there is the fact that although the universe is material in composition, there is nevertheless mental and spiritual activity in it, and there exist such ideas as goodness, justice and love, which hardly developed out of a purely material system; does this not point to the existence of a moral and spiritual being as the creator of the universe (the *moral* argument)?

The nature of the universe thus raises questions about its origin and character. The answers to these questions have been formulated into *arguments* for the existence and nature of God, but there has been immense debate as to whether these arguments actually *prove* anything. The fact is that many thinkers are not persuaded by them, and it can be claimed that an argument which fails to persuade intelligent people is not a compelling argument, since it does not in fact compel assent. On the other hand, it can equally fairly be claimed that counter-arguments intended to disprove the existence of God have not been any more successful. The situation is something of a stalemate. What can be said is that the traditional arguments show that belief in God is not unreasonable, and they help to confirm a belief in God based on other grounds. In the light of other evidence, the universe may be held to constitute one way in which God has revealed himself to us, but the fact remains that the revelation is a somewhat diffuse one taken by itself, and that, at best, it can teach us only a little about the nature of God. Even though Paul believed that creation reveals God, he recognized that men's minds were blind to its significance (Rom. 1:18–23). Clearly we must look for the possibility of other evidence.

Revelation in history (Psalm 78)

We can advance a step further by asking whether there is any evidence of the activity of God in historical events. Is there any way in which the shape of human history reveals the presence of God? This was certainly the belief of the people of Israel. They believed that, so far as their own past was concerned, God had spoken to Abraham and called him to leave his native land and settle in Canaan, where he was to be the ancestor of their nation. After their escape from captivity in Egypt they believed that it was God who brought them out. It was he who raised up Moses to be their leader and who brought them through water and wilderness into the promised land. He gave them their rulers. He provided for their wants. When they did wrong, they saw their disasters as God's judgment on their sins, and when they prospered, they saw this as evidence of

23

God's blessing. Consequently, they spoke of Yahweh (their name for God; mistakenly rendered into English as 'Jehovah') as the living God, meaning that he was active and did things, unlike the dead idols of the pagans.

Here, then, we have a revelation of God which demonstrates his concern for people and displays his moral judgment on the world; this takes us a lot further than revelation in nature. It is not surprising that some theologians stop at this point and suggest that the way God reveals himself is simply by events. Revelation on this view means divine action. The matter, however, is not quite so simple. How do we know which events point to the activity of God, and how do we read off their significance? If you look at the chronicles of the neighbours of Israel, you will find that they looked at the same events, but interpreted them quite differently – if they bothered to interpret them at all. They saw the activity of their gods in some of them, and they would have denied the Israelite interpretation in terms of the activity of Yahweh.

Moreover, we may ask whether this revelation of God is sufficient. A God who merely acts in history is still not a personal God; it is not clear that he can be known by individuals. Our Christian experience (which we may legitimately call into the debate) suggests that there is something more than this to be known about God.

Revelation in Jesus Christ (John 5:19–47)

The coming of Jesus was the supreme manifestation and fulfilment of the revelation which God had begun to make in the life of Israel. Jesus claimed to speak in the name of God and to make known God's will to the people. In his character and actions he revealed the nature of God, and he displayed a righteousness and love which could be seen as a reflection of the character of God. He did mighty works which raised the question whether he was not more than a man, and, most significant of all, after his death his disciples believed that he had come to life again and that they were able to see and speak with him. His followers believed that somehow 'God was in Christ' (2 Cor. 5:19) and they spoke of him as the Word of God.

In Jesus Christ revelation took a personal form. It was no longer a case of merely seeing the effects of God's activity in nature or history. Here, they believed, was God in person, somehow identified with the man Jesus. This was how God communicated with men, by speaking a Word that was in fact a person. Surely this is the supreme revelation of God. And so it is. But once again we face the same question as we faced a moment ago: how do we know that Jesus was a revelation of God? How do we know what God is saying through him? And indeed, to press the point, how do we know what Jesus said and did, since we were not privileged to see him for ourselves? It is not a foolish or irrelevant question, for the simple fact is that people have formed many different ideas about Jesus and his significance. Even if the revelation in Jesus is the *supreme* revelation of God, it is not necessarily a *sufficient* revelation for us.

Revelation in the Bible (Revelation 1)

The answer to the questions which we have been raising is to be found in the existence of the Bible. If we look back at the history of Israel, we find that the significance of that history was expressed by the prophets who claimed to act as the spokesmen of God (1 Sa. 3; Is. 6; Ho. 1; Am. 7:14f.). It was they who revealed to the people that Yahweh's character was righteous and loving (Is. 6:3; Am. 5:6f.; Dt. 7:8; Je. 31:3; Ho. 11:1), that Israel was his chosen people (Dt. 7:7f.; Je. 7:23; 13:11) and that he required of them not only worship, but also righteousness and love in their national and social life (Am. 5:21–24; Is. 1:27; Mi. 6:8). It was through the insights of the prophets and other inspired men that the revelation of God in nature was recognized and expressed (Is. 40; 42:5; Am. 5:8) and that history was seen as the arena of his activity (Dt. 28; Jdg. 2; Am. 5:14; Dn. 2).

The same thing is true of Jesus. We should not have known what he said and did, were it not for the Evangelists who recorded the story. Nor would we have known the significance of Jesus, had it not been for the biblical writers' interpretation of him. Jesus himself drew attention to the way in which the prophets had foretold his coming, so that his life was to be understood in the light of their message (Mt. 5:17; Lk. 24:44). His followers carried the same point further; they realized that the significance of Jesus was that he was the fulfilment of the prophetic message. But above all, they were able to look back on his earthly life in the light of his resurrection and their own Christian experience, and thus to see it in a way that had not been possible earlier. It needed knowledge of the risen Jesus and the Holy Spirit to put the life of Jesus on earth in its full context.

What this means is that our understanding of certain events as revelatory depends on the interpretation of these events by men who were inspired by God to recognize and comment on their significance. In this way the original revelatory events are able to reveal God to later generations (including our own) which did not participate in them, and at the same time the inspired 'commentary' on them is also made available to later men.

We thus find that revelation took place both in events and in the communication of the significance of those events to the biblical writers. Revelation is not a matter of either events or words, but is a combination of both, neither being complete without the other. Obviously a commentary on events that never happened is without revelatory force. But a mere chronicle of events that does not show how they are revelatory is equally useless. The Bible is historical record and explanatory commentary woven into one, and it is because of this dual character that it constitutes God's revelation to us.

In view of this important place which the Bible holds as the means of divine revelation we must now examine its nature in more detail.

The inspiration of the Bible (2 Timothy 3:14–17)

The Bible consists of two parts. In the first we have the record of the first great episode of revelation, God's dealings with Israel. Already by the time of Jesus the Jewish people had come to accept the Old Testament as a set of authoritative documents. There was some doubt about the status of one or two minor books, but substantially the Old Testament existed in its present form. The early Christians naturally accepted this set of books, although it is important to note that they did not accept the unwritten traditions which had developed as well, despite the fact that to some Jews these were every bit as important as the Old Testament. To the Old Testament they added a second part, the records of God's revelation in Jesus and the life of the church. This process of forming the Bible did not take place all at once, but over a long period of time. Although the task was complete in principle by the end of the second century, it is not until AD 367 that we find the first authoritative list of the twenty-seven books of the New Testament as we have them in our Bibles today. The process of forming the 'canon' (or authoritative list) of the books of the Bible was not so much a *conferring* of authority by the church upon these books as a *recognition* of the authority that they inherently possessed.

What exactly was the church doing when it recognized the authority of these books? So far as the Old Testament was concerned, it was simply following the example of Jesus himself and his followers, who accepted these writings as authoritative Scriptures. In the case of the New Testament, it accepted those books which had been used by churches of unquestioned orthodoxy from the earliest days of Christianity and which had been written by the apostles or men (like Mark and Luke) who stood close to them. This test was no formality, for there was a good deal of Christian literature around, some of it of high spiritual content and some positively erroneous, with claims to go back to the early days of the church, and the church had to exercise careful judgment in limiting its Scriptures to those books which actually fulfilled the conditions of canonicity.

The value of these books lay in the fact that they recorded the great acts of God's revelation in the history of Israel and in the ministry of Jesus. At the same time, this record contained the inspired interpretation of these events through which their real meaning could be understood. The Bible is, of course, a human book, written by men, and it bears the marks of the different personalities who contributed to its composition. If it tells how God revealed himself to men, it also records how men responded to God's revelation – and the tale is sometimes one of sorry failure to understand and obey the revelation of God.

At the same time, the Bible is the work of men to whom the Word of God was revealed in various ways. Sometimes the writers were simply recording historical events, using the ordinary means of knowledge to discover what had happened. Sometimes they were recording the messages which prophets and apostles received from God. Sometimes they pondered deeply in their own minds on the things of God and he used their thoughts to bring his message to men. And sometimes they were guided by God to write words that were charged with a deeper meaning than they themselves were aware (1 Pet. 1:10–12; *cf*. Dn. 12:8f.). Although, therefore, the Bible is a set of human books, nevertheless its several writings claim to be divine in origin. Later writers looking back on earlier writings could describe them as 'God-breathed' (2 Tim. 3:16) and state that their authors were men moved by the Holy Spirit (2 Pet. 1:20f.).

This account of the Bible as a book produced under divine inspiration is based on the testimony of its own writers. What reason have we to accept it as a true description, as compared, say, with the claims of the Book of Mormon or the scriptures of other religions? It is clear that a scientific proof of the inspiration of the Bible cannot be attempted. Belief in God is not a matter of accepting a scientific or philosophical proof of his existence; as we have already observed, no such universally accepted proofs exist. Men believe in God because an explanation of their experience in terms of the existence of God is the most satisfying explanation of all the evidence; such belief may go beyond the evidence (as is the case with many hypotheses in other areas of knowledge) and may even go against some of the evidence (such as the existence of pain and suffering); nevertheless, despite the existence of factors that *apparently* militate against belief in God, the believer is prepared to emphasize the word 'apparently', because in his judgment the evidence for belief has greater weight.

Two things follow from this. The first is that, if acceptance of the existence of God is a matter of faith rather than of rigid proof, then acceptance of the Bible as the revelation of God must also be a matter of faith. But this does not mean that acceptance of the Bible is an irrational act without any basis in the evidence, any more than that belief in God is irrational and unjustifiable. The second point is that acceptance of the Bible as the revelation of God must fit in with what we know of God as he has revealed himself. No Christian doubts that in the Bible we have some record of how God has revealed himself in Jesus Christ. The problem is whether it makes sense to claim that the God who revealed himself in Jesus has also revealed himself in a written revelation. Is the Bible itself an inspired revelation of God, or is it merely a human record and interpretation of historical acts of revelation?

Along these lines it has often been argued that written statements can tell us *about* acts of revelation but cannot themselves *be* a revelation, since revelation can occur only through events and persons. The Bible would then be a book about revelation, but not itself a revelation of God. This argument, however, does not do justice to the character of the God who revealed himself in Jesus. He revealed himself as a person. But personal communication takes place by means of words, so much so that one might almost define persons as beings who are able to communicate by means of language. God, therefore, spoke to the prophets by what appeared to them as words (*e.g.* Dt. 4:1–5; 2 Sa. 23:2; Je. 1:9); no doubt the 'words' of an infinite, transcendent God are beyond finite human comprehension, but we may say that God accommodated his forms of expression to what men could receive. Again, when God revealed himself in Jesus, the revelation largely took the form of words. Certainly the Evangelists were as much interested in what Jesus *said* as in what he *did*. According to John, what Jesus said had the character of words of God (Jn. 7:16f.; 8:38; 14:24; 17:8, 14). And when the early church tried to reveal God to people who had not met Jesus for themselves, it did so by *preaching*. Words are an indispensable form of divine communication (*cf.* 1 Cor. 2:13). It follows, therefore, from the character of God as personal, that his revelation of himself had to be in verbal form, as well as in events and persons, and that there is, consequently, nothing surprising about the Christian claim that the Bible is the Word of God in written form. Without a written record the original events by means of which God revealed himself could not be understood in their full significance or be of any revelatory value to later generations which did not experience them.

Some people have suggested that the Bible itself, as originally written, is not the Word of God, but that it can *become* the Word of God as the Spirit of God uses it to speak in new situations to new readers. This view is true in what it positively affirms, namely that the Bible remains a dead letter to the reader if the Spirit does not work in and through it to illumine the mind of the reader. It is false in what it denies, since, for one thing, it is impossible to see how the Bible can become the Word of God if it is not already the Word of God. Furthermore, it is hard to see why the Bible alone has this quality of becoming the Word of God to the reader. Above all, this view does not square with the attitude of Jesus and the New Testament writers to the books of the Old Testament, which they clearly accepted as divine revelation.

People sometimes find it hard to believe that a book written by men could have been inspired by the Spirit of God. We must certainly reject the view that the biblical writers were little more than passive instruments, like typewriters, used by God to record what he wished. There have occasionally been thinkers (like the Jewish writer Philo) who did think of the Scriptures in this way, but it is safe to say that it has been generally repudiated since it does not do justice to the way the biblical writers express it. It would be no more true to say this than to say that Jesus behaved like a divine tape-recorder when he spoke, uttering pre-recorded messages. In fact the biblical writers claim that the word of God came to them in many different ways, but usually through the normal exercise of their God-given faculties of mind and reason.

There is something of a paradox here in that we can regard the Bible as at once a human book and a divine book. But a paradox is not the statement of a contradiction, but rather the expression of two statements which are seemingly contradictory, but contain complementary truths. We have the same kind of paradox in the belief that Jesus was an ordinary man and at the same time the Son of God. Christians firmly hold to this belief although nobody has ever been able to explain it, and indeed it cannot be explained on the level of human understanding, since it is concerned with how the divine can be united with the human. We may legitimately use this analogy to help us to understand the nature of the Bible, provided that we do not fall into bibliolatry, the error of regarding the Bible

31

as a kind of incarnation of the Holy Spirit, and so worshipping it. It is true that some theologians have demurred at the use of the analogy, holding that the inspiration of the Bible is not like the incarnation of the Son of God. And of course they have a point. In the incarnation the second Person of the Trinity became man, but there is no sense in which a divine Person became Scripture. But this is not the point of the analogy, which rather asserts that just as God could be united with man in the incarnation, so God could unite his Word with the words of men in Scripture.

The process of inspiration extends to the Bible as a whole. When the church accepted the canon of Scripture, it was expressly denying the inspiration of other books which dealt with the history of Israel and the early church, but it was equally strongly affirming its conviction that all the books which were accepted were inspired by the Spirit. This does not mean that all books reveal God with the same concentration or the same clarity. There is obviously much more of a divine message in the Gospel of John or in Romans than in Ecclesiastes or the Song of Solomon. But the latter books have important things to say, even if they are peripheral to the central revelation of God in Jesus. We should not forget that the various books of the Bible were written for people in different ages and situations, and a passage that does not speak to us now may have a very relevant message for other people in different circumstances. A letter from a missionary three or four years ago said, 'Give thanks to God for the way in which the Gospel of Mark is helping the people here to see that Christ has overcome the power of the demons'. That was not a lesson that we needed in this country at that time – although since then reports of demon possession and exorcism have demonstrated its relevance here also – but undoubtedly it was and is very relevant indeed for the people in the African country in question.

The reliability and infallibility of the Bible (Luke 1:1–4)

If we say that the Bible as a whole is the inspired Word of God, the obvious implication is that it is a reliable revelation of God. The traditional word for this quality of the Bible is 'infallibility', *i.e.* the quality of not leading people astray. The claim that the Bible is fully reliable is based on the attitude of Jesus to the Old Testament and on the witness of the Bible to its own character (Mt. 5:17f.; Mk. 7:1–13; 12:35–37; Jn. 5:39–47; 10:34–36; 14:26; 16:13–15; 1 Cor. 14:37f.; Eph. 3:3; Rev. 22:6); it is a corollary of the belief that the Bible is inspired by God. Like belief in inspiration, therefore, belief in the reliability of the Bible is a matter of faith and not of proof, but at the same time such belief can be tested by the ordinary methods of historical study.

It is often said that this belief is no longer tenable by modern Christians, and that we cannot believe in the reliability of the Bible because of the many alleged errors and contradictions which it contains. We must therefore state the following points by way of elucidation of this belief.

First, much difficulty has arisen through failure to interpret the Bible correctly. It is a full and reliable revelation of *God*. It is not meant to be a detailed encyclopaedia of factual information on all subjects; it does not profess to provide answers to all the questions that we might want to ask, but to train and instruct us in Christian doctrine and godliness.

Second, the Bible is written in popular language and not with twentieth-century scientific terminology and exactitude. For example, the book of Genesis does not purport to offer a scientific cosmology. Indeed it would be foolish to expect this; and if it had been achieved, not only would it have been unintelligible to the original readers of the Bible, it would also be incomprehensible to most of us who have not had a scientific training.

Third, the Bible records a developing revelation of God

over many centuries to many different people. Its individual statements must be interpreted in the light of the revelation as a whole, and earlier teaching must be related to later teaching. Belief cannot be based on individual statements taken out of their total biblical context. The sacrificial requirements in the Old Testament were true so far as they went, and valid in their own time, but they are no longer a valid expression of God's will for Christians. Even an institution like slavery, which is taken for granted as part of the social system in the New Testament, may no longer be acceptable today in the light of the general ethical teaching of the New Testament itself.

Fourth, so far as the historical truth of the biblical narrative is concerned, archaeology has done a great deal to confirm its essential accuracy, although, in the nature of things, there are many statements for which such confirmation cannot be expected. In general, the basic outline of biblical history can be shown to be dependable, although there are many places where we cannot 'prove' that events took place just as they are recorded, because the required supporting evidence does not exist. It must also be admitted that in some places the biblical narratives raise historical difficulties to which there are at present no convincing answers; in such cases the wisest course may often be to suspend judgment, since fresh discoveries and discussion may alter the situation.

Fifth, many of the alleged difficulties in the Bible are due to our failure to interpret it correctly. The cardinal rule of interpretation is that statements in the Bible must be understood according to the way in which the original writers meant them to be understood. It is folly to take metaphorical or poetic statements as if they were recording literal facts. Passages that were intended to be read as fiction should not be read as if they were historical accounts. It is easy for people of a literal turn of mind to think that all truth must be expressed in literal statements and to forget that truth may be expressed in metaphor and symbol – and that some truths can be expressed only in this way. We cannot, for example, describe the beginning or the end of the universe in literal language, and we should not misunderstand the analogical language used in the Bible in this connection as if it were to be taken literally.

These considerations may help to show that belief in the inspiration and reliability of the Bible can be defended against the arguments customarily brought against it. There are, of course, difficulties about the doctrine, just as there are difficulties surrounding belief in the love of God in a universe where evil and pain occur, but these difficulties are not sufficient to overthrow a doctrine which rests on the teaching of Jesus and his apostles.

Two further points should be made. The first is that, since the Bible is both a human and a divine book, both of these aspects must be taken into consideration in its study. Since it was produced by human writers in particular historical situations, it is both proper and necessary to employ all the usual techniques of historical and literary study in order to place the various books in their historical settings, to discover the circumstances of their composition, and to understand their contents. Such study has sometimes been rejected by Christians on the grounds that it has led to the Bible's being treated as if it were merely a human book, and that it has led to a denial of the truth of the Bible. There is, however, nothing wrong with the methods of study, provided that their use is not vitiated by false presuppositions which call in question the activity of God in revealing himself in the events recorded in the Bible and in the Bible's own statements. If we believe that the Bible is God's Word, we need not fear that critical study is going to disprove it, even though the conclusions of some biblical scholars may appear to contradict its truth.

This points us to the second aspect of the Bible which must not be forgotten in study. The Bible must be read and studied as the Word of God. He who inspired the prophets, apostles and holy men to write the Bible still speaks through it, so that

35

we may come into living contact with him and receive eternal life. When we read the Bible, we must listen to hear his Word, and so we must pray that the Spirit who inspired the writers will illumine the readers to recognize and accept what God is saying to them.

The second point is that the Bible is our final and supreme authority in Christian doctrine and practice. It contains the record of the revelation of Jesus Christ, to which nothing can be added, and it is the book which the church has accepted as canonical and as its final authority in all matters of faith. The purpose of biblical interpretation and theology is not to produce new truths which are not in the Bible, but to bring to light the full meaning of what is already contained in the Bible. It is an essential part of Protestant belief that the church can add nothing to the Bible and that all its doctrines must be tested by their fidelity to the Bible.

There are some questions and problems on which the Bible has nothing specific to say, and in such situations it is the task of the Christian to seek solutions which will be biblical in character and yet may go beyond the teaching of the Bible. Some Christians (though not all) believe, for example, that with the enormous contemporary problems of alcoholism and accidents due to drinking, it is right for them to go beyond the specific commands in the Bible and make their own application of the principle of not causing stumbling blocks (Rom. 14:13, 21) by abstention from alcohol. Other problems arise with practices such as abortion, contraception and euthanasia; here modern techniques and knowledge have raised problems of a kind unknown in biblical times, and Christians have the responsibility of discovering God's will in such areas on the basis of scriptural teaching. These tasks may not be easy, and Christians do not always come to the same conclusions on particular problems; the important thing is to seek solutions which will display obedience to the revealed will of God. Despite its lack of direct teaching on such problems, the Bible contains a sufficient revelation of the will and character of God to enable Christians to know how to believe and act in the modern age.

Questions for study and discussion

1. *If you were trying to persuade a non-Christian of the existence of God, where would you begin?*

2. *Can you trace a pattern in God's dealings with Israel from Psalm 78? Is there any evidence that God still acts on the same principles towards the nations of the world?*

3. *If 'Christ has brought the law to an end', (Rom. 10:4 TEV), what is the place of the Old Testament in a collection of* Christian *Scriptures?*

4. *What objections have been brought against the infallibility of the Bible? Discuss what this term means, and whether the use of it can be defended.*

5. *What principles should we follow in interpreting the Bible as a source of Christian doctrine?*

3

What can we know about God?

A well-known hymn of praise, found in many hymnbooks, opens with the words:

Immortal, invisible, God only wise,
In light inaccessible hid from our eyes.

The rather negative tone with its stress on God's invisibility and unknowability typifies many people's conception of God. Certainly there is a sense in which God *is* incomprehensible and beyond our understanding, and it would be wrong for us to think of him as an 'object' that we can grasp and comprehend like any other object in the universe. But the theme of our previous chapter was that, although man cannot by searching find out God, yet God has revealed himself to us in ways that we can understand. Since man is a creature made in the image of God (Gn. 1:26), it is possible for him to have some understanding of the God who made him. God has revealed himself by means of human language, and so long as we realize that human language is a true, but inadequate, vehicle for communicating the reality of God, we can make some progress in understanding. God has graciously accommodated himself to our feeble and sinful minds by speaking to us in a personal revelation, and so we must remember that the person himself is greater than the revelation. In Jesus we see, as Charles Wesley put it,

Our God contracted to a span,
Incomprehensibly made man.

Provided we remember that he is greater than our understanding, and that human words cannot do justice to him, we can still say much about him.

God in three Persons (Ephesians 1:3–14)

The Bible reveals God to us in three ways. In the Old Testament, particularly, we read about *God the Creator and Lord* of the universe. He alone is God, for the idols of the heathen are in no sense real gods (Ps. 96:5; Is. 45:12–18). On the basis of the teaching in the Old Testament the Jews became convinced monotheists, *i.e.* believers that there is only one God (Mk. 12: 28–34; *cf.* Dt. 6:4).

It was against this background that the early Christians came to believe that *Jesus* shared the nature of God, and we can see that it was a remarkable step for them to take. Jesus himself claimed to come from God and spoke of him in a unique personal sense as his Father (Mt. 11:25–27). When he rose from the dead, Christians saw in this a confirmation of the status which he had claimed for himself, and they said that God had given him the title of 'Lord' (Acts 2:36). The writer of one of the Gospels described him as the *Logos* (Gk. 'word'), a being separate from God and yet called God (Jn. 1:1; *cf.* 20:28). The church knew him as the Son of God (Acts 9:20; Rom. 1:3f.; Gal. 2:20; Heb. 1:1f.); it prayed to him (Acts 7:59; 1 Thes. 3:11ff.); it worshipped him as Lord (Rom. 10:9–13; *cf.* Phil. 2:9–11); and it applied to him titles used of God in the Old Testament (Phil. 2:10f.; *cf.* Rom. 14:10–12 and Is. 45:23; 1 Pet. 2:3; *cf.* Ps. 34:8).

The Old Testament contained references to the *Spirit of God* as one of the means by which God spoke and acted in the world. This Being was more fully revealed in New Testament times. He was spoken of as 'another comforter' (*i.e.* 'strength-ener' or 'advocate') sent from God to take the place of Jesus with his followers after the ascension (Jn. 14:16f., 26; 16:7–11, 13–15, 26). He was described in personal terms (Rom. 8:26f.; 15:30; 1 Cor. 12:11; Eph. 4:30; 1 Tim. 4:1) and regarded as divine (2 Cor. 3:17f.).

The striking thing is the way in which the earliest Christian writings name God the Father and Jesus his Son alongside each other (Gal. 1:3; 1 Thes. 1:1) in a way that must have shocked the Jews with their belief in the uniqueness of God the Father. The Holy Spirit too was linked with the Father and Son in a way which suggests irresistibly that all three Beings stood on the same level (Mt. 28:19; 2 Cor. 13:14; Eph. 2:18; 4:4–6; 2 Thes. 2:13f.; 1 Pet. 1:1f.). The actual term 'God', however, is rarely used directly of Jesus and never of the Spirit.

This understanding of the Father, Son and Spirit arose out of Christian experience as God revealed himself in Jesus and then in the life of the church, and the New Testament writers seem to have accepted it without thinking too deeply about its implications. But the problem was inevitable: how could this belief in three divine Persons be reconciled with the Old Testament idea of only one God? During the first two or three centuries of Christian history many attempts were made to solve this problem. Various solutions were tried which proved inadequate. One solution was to suggest that the Father alone was God and that the Son and Spirit were lesser, created beings, superior-quality angels, so to speak. Another suggestion was that 'Father', 'Son' and 'Spirit' were three roles played by God, rather like one actor appearing in three different parts in a play. Neither of these solutions did justice, however, to the plain facts revealed in the New Testament, namely that the three Persons were each fully God, and that God was at one and the same time existent as three Persons.

It is doubtful whether the problem of the being of God can

be solved in the sense of giving an explanation of it. Christians have been content to affirm the doctrine in a form which takes account of all the facts and to try to find human analogies which may throw some light on it.

Some people find these analogies helpful, although obviously none of them must be pressed too far. All of them start from the point that the biblical teaching reveals one God (the basic Old Testament doctrine) who is nevertheless revealed in a threefold way (the New Testament revelation). The problem is then to state how one God can combine unity and diversity. At an impersonal level we may think of how an atom is a unity composed of various kinds of particles. A biological organism consists of a unity of different indispensable parts. The human personality unites intelligence, feeling and will in such a way that we can hardly conceive of the whole without its parts or the parts without the whole. Other analogies have been drawn from personal relationships. Thus a husband and wife who are bound together by the closest ties of love can be one in thought and purpose and yet are clearly capable of independent action, which is nevertheless in harmony with the wills of both of them. In the same way, Jesus spoke of his relationship as a Son to the Father in terms of mutual knowledge and a common purpose (Jn. 5:19f.; 17:21, 23).

These two types of analogy may be of some help. The former emphasizes the unity and the latter the distinctness of the parts of the whole. Together they point to the need to stress the oneness of God and the distinctness of the Father, Son and Spirit. The term which has come to be used for the three members of the Godhead is 'Persons'. Whatever its original meaning – which was more that of the 'roles' played by actors – it inevitably conveys to modern readers all that is meant by human personality. This development in usage is understandable and legitimate. Father, Son and Spirit do each show the characteristics which we associate with human person-hood, and in particular the capacity to enter into relationships with other persons. It may be most helpful to think of the Trinity as a unity of three Persons, joined by the closest ties of love and common purpose, so that they appear as one God. This is certainly suggested by the way in which Jesus is regarded as the Son of the Father. This way of speaking was misunderstood in the early church to mean that the Son was 'begotten' by the Father at some remote point in time past, but it was generally realized that to say this was to press the metaphor of human fatherhood further than was legitimate; what it means is that the Son stands in a perpetual relation of sonship to the Father. The Bible does not offer any comparable way of speaking about the relation of the Spirit to the Father, but the early church developed the thought that the Spirit 'proceeded' from the Father and the Son (*cf*. Jn. 15:26). This manner of speaking states the relationship without explaining it.

To speak of God as the Trinity is to affirm that he exists as one God and yet in three Persons, all equally divine.

God is spirit (John 4:24)

The basis of the biblical understanding of God is the doctrine of the Trinity. Our next step must be to consider the character of the God who is revealed to us in this threefold manner. We shall base our discussion on a series of affirmations made by John in his Gospel and First Epistle. These affirmations were not meant as a systematic and comprehensive summary of the nature of God, but nevertheless they do offer a very handy summary of the biblical teaching.

The first, and most difficult, of these affirmations is that God is spirit. The difficulty is obviously that we have just spoken of one particular Person of the Trinity as 'the Spirit' and now we have to affirm that this word applies to the Father also. At the same time the word is popularly used of the soul of a man as distinct from his body, or of the life-breath which animates his body, or of superhuman beings. In general, the word is used of non-material beings, and it is this idea that is present when we speak of God as spirit. His manner of existence is basically different from our human bodily existence (*cf*. Is. 31:3).

On the negative side, this warns us against thinking falsely of God as having a human or material body like the superhuman figures of Greek gods. He is not to be confused in any way with man-made idols, and the Bible strongly forbids any attempt to make material representations of him (Ex. 20:4-6). Any such representations are bound to be crude and misleading. Our normal physical and material ways of thinking completely break down when they are applied to God.

On the positive side, the term 'spirit' implies that God's existence is on a higher level than ours. It is true, real existence, free from the limitations and corruption associated with bodily existence. The idea that God is free from physical limitations, and so is all-knowing, all-powerful and all-present, is bound up with the thought that he is spirit. In John 4:24 spirit and truth are closely associated. What is spiritual is therefore ultimately real and lasting. God is eternal spirit.

God is love (1 John 4:8)

God as spirit is the basis of reality and truth. These qualities come into clearer focus when we consider the biblical revelation of his character as loving. Love involves at least two people, the lover and the beloved. The Bible makes it clear that the Father and Son are bound together by mutual love (Jn. 5:20; Col. 1:13), and it is reasonable to conclude that the Holy Spirit shares in this loving activity although the Bible does not explicitly state this. God's love for the world is then an extension of this eternal loving relationship within the Trinity so as to include the world, and human love is meant to be a copy of this love (1 Jn. 4:11).

But love is a word with several different meanings, and it is important to understand what the term means when it is used of God. There are at least two Greek words translated into English as love. One is the word *erōs* which often expresses the desire to have or possess the object which one loves and so to obtain pleasure and satisfaction. Such love is called forth by the sheer desirableness of its object, and its aim is essentially selfish; it aims primarily at its own good, and its watchword is 'get'. This word is not used in the Bible. The other word is *agapē*. The kind of love often expressed by this word aims to give pleasure and satisfaction to the object of its affection, rather than to the lover. It does not simply love the lovable but it reaches out to the unlovely and unlovable and makes it lovable. It is fundamentally unselfish and altruistic, it aims at the good of the beloved, and its watchword is 'give'. Naturally this does not mean that the lover himself gets no satisfaction or pleasure out of his love. His satisfaction is that which comes from giving to others and sharing their joy, and of course the *agapē* of one person can be matched by the answering *agapē* of another.

There are other concepts of love as well as these (see C. S. Lewis, *The Four Loves*), but this comparison of the two concepts of love which have come to be broadly associated with these two Greek words will suffice to make our point. The kind of love which is shown by God is *agapē*. It is this word that is used in the Bible for his love, and it is fair to say that the concept of giving love largely developed from the use of this word in the Greek translation of the Old Testament to describe the love of God. We might go so far as to say that men arrived at this concept of love only from seeing what love meant in the case of God. The idea of love as giving, in distinction from desire or friendship, is bound up with the revelation of God's character. 'God shows his love for us in that while we were yet sinners Christ died for us' (Rom. 5:8). 'In this is love, not that we loved God but that he loved us and sent his Son to be the expiation for our sins' (1 Jn. 4:10). These two verses sum up the matter. God's love is concerned with the welfare of the undeserving and confers benefit on those who have no title to it nor show any love to him. Human love is possibly never free from self-seeking. God's love is given freely to all men without discrimination and seeks only their highest good. Here is the pattern for a human love which cares for all men regardless of their race, colour, language or place in society.

This, then, is the kind of love which is shown in the fellowship of the three Persons of the Godhead. It led to the creation of the universe, and it brought the Son of God to earth to win back rebellious mankind into joyful fellowship with God. It is this love which lies behind the ascription of the title of Father to God. He is Father primarily of Jesus as his Son (Jn. 5:20). It is very significant that the Bible scarcely ever uses the term 'father' of God's relationship to mankind in general. It is only when men respond to his redeeming love and become his spiritual children (Mt. 6:9, 15) that they enter into a family relationship with him; only then are they entitled to call him their Father. The popular modern idea that God is the Father of all men and that they can expect all the privileges of his fatherly goodness without undertaking any filial responsibilities has no basis in biblical teaching and needs to be clearly exposed as an error. If God's love is available for all mankind, it remains true that entry into a relationship in which he is known as Father is reserved for those who are prepared to respond positively and wholeheartedly to his invitation.

God is light (1 John 1:5)

In the Bible light is a symbol for various ideas, such as holiness, goodness, truth, knowledge and salvation. It is thus a natural symbol for God, who is the supreme embodiment of these qualities (Ps. 27:1; Mal. 4:2; Jn. 3:19; 8:12; 2 Cor. 6:14; Eph. 5:8f.; Rev. 22:5).

God's character as light can express his separateness from

45

men (1 Tim. 6:16), but it can also signify that he gives guidance and direction to men in the darkness of this world (1 Jn. 2:8–11). Above all the symbolism of light in its purity speaks of the holiness of God. We should not distinguish this attribute of God too sharply from his love, as if these were two different aspects of his character. The temptation for some thinkers has been to regard holiness as almost the opposite of love, if not actually incompatible with it. It makes better sense to say that holiness and love are like the obverse and reverse sides of the same coin. They are two complementary, personal aspects of the character of God.

It has been said that holiness is what makes God different from man, and certainly something of the mystery and majesty of God is summed up in this word. But at the heart of God's holiness there lies the moral quality of righteousness. He is just in all his ways. Justice can be understood negatively in terms of treating people as they deserve, and, in particular, of meting out the appropriate punishment to a wrong-doer. God's justice, however, is predominantly positive, for it expresses itself primarily in love and mercy even to the undeserving. Justice means seeing that people get what they deserve when good things are being handed out, as well as that penalties are given to those who deserve them. The gospel itself can be regarded as a revelation of the righteousness of God (Rom. 1:17). It is precisely *because* he is faithful and just that he forgives the penitent sinner (1 Jn. 1:9). He is a righteous God and *therefore* a Saviour (Is. 45:21). God's love is righteous love, so that it is not a matter of arbitrary sentiment; his righteousness is loving righteousness, so that it is not a matter of austere payment of what is owed. True love is seen in justice, and true justice in love.

The concrete expression of God's holiness and righteousness is the moral law, which he has given to men as the way of life they must follow. Love is meant to express itself in harmonious relationships. Just as the life of the triune God is marked by

46

perfect harmony, so the life of man in his relationships with his fellow men and with God should be marked by harmony. This means that there must be some rules regarding the expression of love in human relationships. The essence of God's law is accordingly that men ought to love God and one another (Mk. 12:29-31). This basic law, however, needs to be expanded into a great number of commandments which express the obligations of love in different circumstances.

These commandments are given to men in the context of God's love and concern for them. In the Old Testament they mostly appear as part of the covenant made by God with the people of Israel. They were spoken in the context of God's love for the people, expressed in his deliverance of them from their slavery in Egypt. He summoned them to be his people and promised his fatherly care, on condition that they would obey his commands. Similarly, in the New Testament the concrete instructions for daily life appear in the form of an explanation of what it means to respond to the love of God revealed in Jesus. This does not mean, however, that God's commands are binding solely on those who agree to accept his covenant and grace. Ultimately they express his will as the creator of mankind, and they are rooted in the moral law which finds its source in him. If this way of life is not followed by men, the consequence is the breakdown of life itself; human relationships become destroyed and the life of men together fails to achieve its purpose. The tragedy is that men have refused to acknowledge the demands of God's love expressed in his law. They would prefer to be free from it, and they imagine that their way is better. When love is thus denied the possibility of existence, God's holiness is felt as an alien force, and it cannot be experienced in any other way than in wrath and judgment.

When men refuse to accept God's way, they become the objects of his wrath. This is the inevitable consequence of their attitude, since there can be no room in a moral universe governed by the law of love for those who live for themselves and refuse to submit to the law which structures the universe. If a man rejects the holy demands and the loving offers of God, he himself must be rejected and suffer exclusion from the presence and life-giving power of God, as the penalty of his rebellion (Mt. 25:31ff.; 2 Thes. 1:3–12).

This is why God's holiness symbolizes his separation from men. It is not because of their finiteness that men are separated from God. It is because of their sin that they exclude themselves from him, for no sinner can stand in the presence of God (Mal. 3:1f.). The Bible implies that if it were not for their sinfulness, men could enjoy fellowship with their Creator (*cf.* Gn. 2:8; 5:22–24; Ex. 33:11). This fellowship has been destroyed by sin, and God's holiness is now a barrier to the approach of sinners into his presence. But God himself has taken the initiative in reopening a way to fellowship through the gospel (1 Jn. 1:3, 7). He wants men to come back into fellowship with him and to share his holy nature (2 Pet. 1:3–11), and so he gives himself freely in love, bearing their sin and taking its evil effects upon himself in order that they might be freed from it and be fit to come into his presence. It is the very greatness of this holy love which makes the sin of men in rejecting him all the more heinous and culpable.

Questions for study and discussion

1. *On the basis of such a passage as Ephesians 1:3–14, what would you say is the significance of the doctrine of the Trinity for the Christian in his spiritual life?*

2. *Do you think that it is fitting to address prayers to the Son or the Spirit as well as to the Father?*

3. *With the aid of a concordance examine the teaching of the New Testament about God as* Father *: what evidence, if any, is there that he is the Father of all mankind?*

4. *'The divine attributes of justice and mercy . . . do not need to be reconciled, for they are never at war' (J. Denney) : discuss.*

5. *Make a list of the different kinds of human love. What light do they throw on the nature of God's love?*

4

God and the universe

The story which runs through the Bible from Genesis to Revelation is the story of how God created the world, how the world fell into sin and rebellion against him, and how God has begun a process of new creation which will continue until every trace of sin has been destroyed. In the present chapter we are to look at the creation of the universe and then, more closely, at the nature of man and how he fell into sin.

God the Creator (Genesis 1)

The way in which the Bible describes the creation of the world can best be appreciated by a comparison with two other types of approach. On the one hand, many ancient cultures possessed stories describing how the gods made the universe in some crude fashion. The Babylonian epic of creation describes how the god Marduk slays the rebel Tiamat, and then fillets her body like that of a fish, using one half to make the sky and the other half to make the earth. Although some superficial resemblances can be traced between the biblical accounts of creation and these pagan stories, it is abundantly clear that the former are remarkably free from the mythological elements and sheer fantasy found in the culture of Israel's neighbours, and are altogether on a loftier, monotheistic level of thought.

On the other hand, we have the kind of explanation of the origins of the universe found in a modern textbook of scientific cosmology. The Bible makes no attempt to give an account of this kind, and it would have been impossible for it to do so. A typical modern book on cosmology outlines several competing theories on the subject and expresses them in a mathematical form which is beyond the ordinary reader's comprehension. Had the Bible attempted to provide a scientific cosmology it would doubtless have been equally beyond the understanding of the ordinary person.

Instead, the biblical account gives us a poetic description of the fact that God created the universe; it lists what can be seen in the world and asserts that everything owes its origin to God. It makes no attempt to explain how God created the world, and indeed it is doubtful whether the act of creation could be described in words.

It is a misunderstanding of the account in Genesis 1 to see it as a scientific account of what happened. Hence the alleged conflicts between the biblical account and modern scientific accounts of creation are merely apparent. The two types of account are doing two different, complementary tasks. The scientist is interested in the 'what' and 'how' of the universe; he wants to describe it accurately and explain the laws which governed its development. The Bible is interested in the 'why' of the universe, with the questions of its ultimate origin, final destiny and moral significance. These are two different questions, and attempts to answer them need not produce any conflict, so long as theologians and scientists do not make illegitimate attempts to answer each other's questions. It is true that there is a certain 'no man's land' between science and theology, where real problems can arise, but the work of many scientists who are also Christians suggests that these problems are capable of a coherent Christian solution.

The purpose of the biblical account of creation is, then, to teach that the universe is not self-existent but owes its origin to God. Pagan myths, such as the Babylonian one quoted above, suggest that the gods created the universe out of some previously existing 'stuff', just as a potter imposes an intelligible form on a shapeless lump of clay. By contrast the Bible asserts emphatically that God created the universe out of nothing (*ex nihilo*). He created the materials as well as moulded them to shape (Heb. 11:3). We may even suggest that space and time are his creation, although since we cannot think without making use of the framework of space and time it is impossible for us to imagine what the creation of these might mean.

The biblical doctrine of creation rules out the view which is still often found that God is to be wholly or partly identified with the universe. The ancient philosophical system of *pantheism* has no support in the Bible, which emphasizes that the universe is merely the creature made by God. God is far greater than the universe which he created and over which he rules. No matter how great the universe may be, he inhabits eternity and the earth is like a mere footstool to him (Is. 57:15; 66:1). This is why the Bible is so vehemently opposed to idolatry, which is the worship of the creation, or part of the creation, rather than the Creator (Rom. 1:25). In modern times some astronauts have commented that they did not see God in the course of their explorations, and one might be tempted to draw the foolish conclusion that there is no God. Such a view fails to recognize the *transcendence* of God as the One who is greater than the universe and whose existence is not bound by our categories of space and time.

The popular view of creation posits an act of God at some point in the remote past which brought the universe into being and, as it were, set it going like a clock to carry on ticking under its own power without any further attention. This view is open to criticism on three accounts. It makes God into a kind of absentee landlord who has left his universe to its own devices and no longer exercises any control over it; this is the error known as *deism* which flourished in the eighteenth century. It also fails to take into account the possibility of the continual replenishment of the universe with fresh supplies of matter –

the so-called 'continuous creation' of matter, postulated by some cosmologists. Further, it ignores the continuous creation of new forms of inanimate and animate nature that surround us at every turn. The question, 'Who made this beautiful scene?' is not completely answered by speaking about God's original act of creation: we need to refer to the action of wind and water over centuries, to the planting or removal of vegetation by human agencies, and so on. Similarly, when a child asks, 'Who made me?' it was not the original act of creation by God that was responsible but the coming together of his parents in a creative union. It follows that our doctrine of creation must preserve the insight that God continues to create the universe in and through such natural acts. He exercises continual care and control over the universe, and if he did not do so, it would cease to exist (cf. Col. 1:17).

When we turn to the New Testament we find that Jesus Christ is closely linked with God the Father in the work of creation. He is clearly the central agent in the new creation which is the theme of the New Testament, but he was also involved in the original creation of the universe (Heb. 1:1–3). A careful distinction is made between the roles of the three Persons of the Trinity. God the Father is the ultimate author of creation. His Son is the agent by whom the world was created, and he is said to be the one for whom it exists (1 Cor. 8:6). The Spirit is also associated with the creation (Gn. 1:2). Thus, as we might expect, the whole Trinity is involved in the work of creation.

God the Lord (Psalms 107; 148)

If God created the universe, he must be greater than it. It is not surprising, therefore, that he is spoken of as the Lord or Sovereign of all that he has created. This relationship is expressed by the three 'omni-' words which bring out the supreme authority of God over the whole of creation.

God is *omnipotent* or all-powerful. He is able to do what he wishes to do (*cf.* Is. 40:21–31). Of course, this does not mean that he is able to do things which are self-contradictory or absurd. People have sometimes poured scorn on the Christian belief in the omnipotence of God by asking, 'Can God create a stone so heavy that even he cannot lift it?' We need not waste our time over logical puzzles of this kind. Rather we should be moved to wonder at the power by which God the Son was able to become part of his own creation when he was incarnate as a man. From the point of view of logic this too is an impossibility, but our inability to comprehend how it is possible reflects the finiteness of our human understanding. A much more important problem in relation to God's sovereignty is the existence of evil in the world (see the last section of this chapter).

God is *omniscient* or all-knowing. He fully knows and understands the universe which he has created. Nothing that happens in it is hidden from his sight (*cf.* Rom. 11:33–36; Col. 2:3). Here again we have a concept which transcends what our minds can conceive. It is not possible for us to imagine a situation in which we know everything, including all that we ourselves are going to do. The Bible speaks of God's fore-ordaining of what is going to happen in the future, so that history proceeds according to his plan and his prophets are able to foretell certain aspects of what is going to happen. Such fore-ordination necessarily includes what God himself is going to do in the future. But as soon as we try to think of what is implied in a free agent fore-ordaining what he himself is going to do in the future, we find that we involve ourselves in a logical tangle from which there is no escape. Omniscience is an attribute of God which we can confess, but cannot understand. This is why the concept of predestination, which has played so important a part in Protestant theology, must be handled with the greatest care. To speak of God's omniscience and predestination is to speak of a mystery, which lies beyond human comprehension, and from which we can easily draw false conclusions. Rather we use

54

these words to confess the greatness of the God to whom we can commit our future in entire confidence that he will work all things for our good (Rom. 8:28).

God is *omnipresent* or all-present. This too is a quality which can be misunderstood and can be the cause of problems. We are obviously not to think of God as being like some kind of rarefied gas or wireless waves filling all space. Rather the point is that no part of the universe is closed from God and his activity. Jacob found that he could not escape from the watchful eye of God by running away from home (Gn. 28:10ff., especially verse 16), and a psalmist affirmed that it is impossible to flee from God by day or by night, in life or in death (Ps. 139). Men may find God and commune with him anywhere and at any time (Mt. 28:20). The doctrine of omnipresence is thus an expression of the fact that God is always there to help his people with sovereign power. Nevertheless, it is possible to speak of men shutting themselves off from the presence of God by their sin, and we sometimes talk as though there were degrees of God's presence: the saying of Jesus about his being present when two or three gather in his name (Mt. 18:20) suggests that he is present in a special way in groups of Christians, although we would not want to deny that he can be fully present with the individual Christian. The term 'presence' is somewhat open-textured and can have a somewhat different force in different contexts.

The effect of speaking of God in terms of these three rather abstract concepts is thus to bring out the greatness and wisdom of his care for his people, which is available to them at all times and everywhere. This care of God for the universe and its inhabitants has traditionally found expression in the term *providence* (literally, 'foresight'). The biblical writers ascribe the round of the seasons, the provision of rain and sunshine, and all that enables man to live in security, to God's gracious care for the world. This care is related to the behaviour of God's people. The Old Testament story shows that when Israel was righteous she enjoyed prosperity on the material level, but when she served false gods and ceased to trust God to provide for her, disaster followed (Gn. 1:29f.; 8:22; Dt. 28; Ps. 104; Mt. 6:25–34; 10:29–31).

It must be admitted that there is not an exact correspondence between human behaviour and divine provision for human needs. We cannot trace connections between human piety and material prosperity and between human sin and natural disasters in the way the Old Testament prophets did; lacking their prophetic insight, it would be quite wrong for us to say that some particular natural disaster was due to some particular sinful act on the part of man. The biblical writers themselves were very conscious of the problem that the wicked often seem to prosper at the expense of the righteous and were driven to the conclusion that the problem can be solved only when what happens after death is taken into consideration (Pss. 49; 73). It is here that the character of religious faith as *faith* is relevant. Faith is not, as the schoolboy definition once put it, 'believing what you know isn't true'. It is, however, believing despite considerable obstacles that something is true. The appearances are often against Christian belief, and we are tempted to an interpretation of the universe which sees only its outward character of confusion; faith is the daring act by which, in virtue of such stubborn facts as the life, death and resurrection of Jesus, we are not content with mere appearances but believe that behind the universe there stands the figure of a loving and all-powerful God. The Christian belief is that, no matter how great be the tribulations of the man who trusts in God, nevertheless God knows his situation, cares for him in the midst of it, and will eventually bring him safely through.

The nature of man (Psalm 8)

Man is the climax and crown of God's creation, for, unlike other creatures, he is the image of God (Gn. 1:26f.). This

56

phrase means that he is like God and in some way is God's representative in the world. He has dominion over the world of nature, and is able to control his environment and create new things. Above all, he possesses a moral nature. Alone of created beings he is capable of moral behaviour; he knows the difference between right and wrong, between love and hatred. He is capable of fellowship with other men and with God himself. He is a being with a moral and spiritual nature that distinguishes him from the rest of creation and places him 'a little lower than God', yet firmly as a creature.

The Bible's description of man as a creature made to be God's image is unaffected by scientific questions regarding the origin of the human race. There has been much debate among Christians about the correctness or otherwise of the theory of biological evolution, and some would argue that the theory cannot be true because it contradicts the biblical account of the special creation of man. A number of questions can easily be confused here, as with the general question of the creation of the universe. It must be insisted that the question of the biological beginnings of the human species is a question for the scientist and cannot be settled by an appeal to the Bible. The Bible is not concerned to give a scientific account of the origin of man, but to insist on his divine creation and his spiritual nature. There is no necessary conflict between the Bible and science, provided that we do not interpret the biblical account of creation in a literalistic manner which goes against the intention of the original writer. Again, we do well to remember that biological evolution remains a scientific hypothesis, admittedly the most generally accepted theory, but, like every scientific hypothesis, open to falsification and replacement by a better theory. Further, assertions about the spiritual nature of man cannot be falsified by appeal to his possible humble origins, any more than a pearl can be said to be worthless because it comes out of a humble oyster. In the same way a man's worth is not to be measured by his chemical ingredients (once valued at £1, but inflation has affected the figure somewhat), but by his spiritual, moral and physical qualities. The trouble is that we think too exclusively of Adam as being made in God's image; but so too is every child born to human parents. The statement that man is God's image is a statement about us all, and not merely about the first man.

Just as the biblical account of the origin of man is not meant to be a scientific statement, so too the biblical description of the nature of man is not meant to be a scientific statement of this. It is in fact dangerous to construct a biblical 'psychology', because the same psychological terms are used by the different biblical authors with varying shades of meaning. In general, however, we can say that in the Old Testament man is regarded as a creature made of flesh and bones; he is described as being a living soul, and his life is inbreathed by God (*e.g.* 2 Sa. 19:12f.; Gn. 2:7). In the New Testament man has a body composed of flesh and blood (1 Cor. 15:50), and he has, or is, a soul (*psychē*) and a spirit (*pneuma*) (1 Thes. 5:23). It is an old argument whether man is correspondingly bipartite (body and soul) or tripartite (body, soul and spirit). The tendency among modern scholars is to say that these three words refer to three different, but closely related, aspects of man; 'body' refers to him as a physical being, 'soul' to him as a being who has a mental life, and 'spirit' to him as a being who has a spiritual life. Rather than his having three 'parts', he can be looked at from three different points of view. Nevertheless, the term 'body' appears to refer to the physical aspect of man rather than to his whole being, and the term 'soul' or 'spirit' refers to his mental and spiritual aspect rather than to his whole being.

The chief purpose of man's creation has been expressed briefly and memorably in the Westminster Shorter Catechism as 'to glorify God, and to enjoy him for ever'. Manifestly this statement needs to be filled out, concerned as it is solely with man's relation to God. But it has the merit of putting first things first by stating that man's life is meant to be centred on God, to be devoted to the praise of God (both in actual words and also in its general motivation), and to find its supreme joy in living fellowship with God. It is the merit of John Calvin to have rediscovered this central truth, that God is at the centre, and man is his creation. In a justly famous passage in his *Reply to Sadolet* he criticized the Roman Catholic theology of his day for placing too much stress on man and his desires for eternal blessedness, as if this should be man's chief interest: 'it is not very sound theology to confine a man's thoughts so much to himself, and not to set before him as the prime motive of his existence zeal to show forth the glory of God. For we are born first of all for God, and not for ourselves'. It is not too much to say that this placing of God at the centre and man in subordination to him is the fundamental insight of Calvin's theology and of Protestant theology generally.

At the same time, man is made to live in community with his fellow men, the basic unit being the family, which reflects the Father-Son relationship in the Trinity (*cf.* Eph. 3:15). It is virtually impossible for man to live without some kind of community – the Robinson Crusoe type of situation is highly unusual and manifestly incomplete – and it is only in community that he can fully realize his nature as a person. Indeed it could be said that 'person' is a term which involves reciprocal relationships, just like 'husband' or 'wife'.

The problem of evil (Genesis 3; Job 24)

So far we have been looking at the universe and man in relation to their Creator without taking into account the complications caused by the existence of sin and evil. According to the familiar biblical story, however, the creation of man was quickly followed by the entry of evil into his heart. He was created with the possibility of choosing between right and wrong, between obedience to God and disobedience. But he made the wrong decision at the instigation of the tempter, and sin with all its dreadful consequences entered the world (Gn. 3: *cf*. Rom. 5:12-21; 2 Cor. 11:3).

The story of Adam and Eve's fall is concerned only with the fact of sin's entry into mankind. We are not told how or why evil arose. The temptation comes from the serpent who was apparently one of the creatures made by God, but we are not told how it came to have its evil nature in a world which God created 'very good'. Other passages in the Old Testament push back the story of evil by suggesting some kind of disobedience among angelic beings before the creation of the world (*cf*. Gn. 6:1-8; Is. 14:12-15; Ezk. 28:12-19; Jude 6), but these too do not offer us any explanation of how sin arose.

The problem of sin, *i.e.* human wrongdoing, is closely bound up with the problem of evil generally. Evil is anything that causes pain and suffering and interferes with the enjoyment of life. Men suffer through a variety of causes, including their own wicked actions and those of their fellow men, but also through natural calamities, such as storms and earthquakes, deadly bacteria and poisons. Much suffering is caused by ignorance, some but not all of which might have been avoided. The nature of man as a being subject to decay also leads to suffering and eventually to death. There is suffering too in the animal world, although we may perhaps exaggerate its conscious extent in animals with elementary nervous systems.

Such suffering is obviously not in proportion to the personal wickedness of men, so that it might be regarded as due retribution for their evil ways. Indeed, it is its haphazardness that makes it so hard to bear. To a certain extent men can bear pain when they can see a reason for it: a person is ready to suffer aching muscles and a racing heart in order to achieve some feat of physical endurance. We recognize that some pain is inevitable in the world. But there still remain the two basic problems of the existence of much pain and suffering that seems to serve no useful end, to spoil life rather than to ennoble it, and of the sheer arbitrariness of it all. 'Why does it happen to *me*?' is perhaps the most characteristic and pressing question asked by the sufferer. The thoughtful person may produce the even more baffling question: 'If God is good and all-powerful, why cannot he arrange things so as to avoid suffering and evil?' If we reply that suffering is due to human sinfulness, this still does not explain the existence of natural calamities, nor does it deal with the objection that God could have created beings who, although possessed of freewill (or the appearance of it), are so controlled by him as to avoid falling into sin and suffering.

It is possible to advance various points which mitigate the difficulty of these questions, such as the warning value of certain experiences of pain (*e.g.* toothache) or the good effects on character produced by undergoing some painful disciplines; but it should be emphasized that some people speak far too casually of the good effects of suffering, and forget that warning pains are warnings against worse pains, and that certain types of suffering (such as the effects of rabies or brain damage) cannot by any stretch of the imagination be regarded as means of refining the character of the sufferers.

Other types of solution may be suggested which limit either the goodness or the power of God, so that he is either unwilling or unable to deal with the problem. Such solutions (particularly the latter one) may lead to a dualistic view of the universe in which God is opposed by an evil power. Christians have almost universally rejected such a solution, since the postulation of two equally powerful opposing forces leaves it uncertain which is going to win in the end and puts a large question mark against the biblical assertions of God's sovereignty. On the other hand, it seems even more difficult to trace the origin of evil to the will of God, and the Bible categorically denies this idea (Gn. 1:31; Jas. 1:13; such a passage as Is. 45:7 simply asserts that God sends calamity upon men as a penalty for their sins).

One solution is to argue that God permits evil rather than directly wills it, but this does not solve the problem, because to speak of 'permitting' is to imply that God himself would prefer that things were other than they actually are. Or, it may be argued, what appears evil and pointless to us would nevertheless appear good and purposeful could we see it from God's angle with a fuller knowledge than we can possess as men. Job is the classical example of the man who could not see the reason for his sufferings, although the reason is revealed to the readers of his story, and the point of the book is that, if the sufferer had known why he was suffering, his sufferings would have lost their purpose of demonstrating to Satan Job's resolute faith in God.

Yet another type of solution is to argue that the problem arises because of the creation of man as a person with freewill to respond to God in love. Such freedom implies the possibility of refusal to love God and carries with it the risk of all the attendant suffering. But this solution means that God still permits the development of evil in the world, even if he does not approve of it. Nor does it solve the problem of natural calamities which cannot be ascribed to the results of human rebellion against God.

The truth of the matter seems to be that evil is an irrational quantity in the universe, a surd which cannot be either explained or explained away. The Bible does not explain its origin, and its origin cannot be explained; perhaps if it could be explained, it would cease to be evil. What the Bible does say is, first, that God is implacably opposed to evil, so that he is not to be regarded as its origin; second, that God is active to overcome evil and that he has demonstrated this supremely by himself submitting to its effects in the death of Jesus; third, that God is mightier than evil, a fact which he showed in raising Jesus from the dead and which will be shown in his final victory.

There are difficulties in ascribing the origin of evil to God or to an independent power; we must be content to leave its origin a mystery. Its existence continues to be the biggest objection that can be brought against the Christian belief in God. The objection, however, is far from decisive, although it must be continually assessed and answered. It can be rebutted by the Christian understanding of the cross as the event in which God has declared his opposition to sin and his involvement up to the hilt in sharing the suffering of mankind and enabling them to overcome it. The Christian may also want to suggest that the non-believer has an even greater problem in explaining the presence of good and beautiful things in a purely material universe.

The nature and effects of sin (Romans 1:18–2:16)

However mysterious the origin of sin, its character in the lives of men is all too obvious. We can describe it from three points of view, in relation to God, other people and the sinner himself.

In relation to God, sin is *rebellion* against him. It is dis-obedience to his will and purpose expressed in the command-ments he has given to men (Dt. 17:2; 1 Ki. 8:50; Is. 1:2; 63:10). The sinner is a person who misses the mark by falling short of God's standards for human conduct (Lk. 15:18, 21; Rom 3:23). Instead of giving God the worship and love due to him, he offers his devotion to other gods; in the ancient world this was expressed in idolatry, but in both the ancient and the modern worlds the essence of idolatry is to make something other than God the object of one's supreme concern and passion (Ex. 20:3–6; Lk. 12:13–21; 1 Cor. 10:14–22). Sin is basically a refusal to accept God as our sovereign Lord, and it often expresses itself in a perverted knowledge of him which denies his truth and love (Rom 1:18–23; 2 Cor. 4:4).

In relation to our fellow-men, sin is seen in *immorality*, *injustice* and *lack of love* (Rom 1:18–32: 13:9f.; 1 Jn. 3:15; 4:8). These words all indicate the attitude which refuses to treat other people as persons with their own rights. The sinner refuses to respect the rights of other people and disrupts the fellowship of love, which is God's purpose for men. He treats other people as means rather than as ends, as things which he can use for his own pleasure instead of as persons who are to be helped to enjoy fullness of life. He is like a child playing a game, who is determined that he shall win at any price and disobeys the rules in order to beat his competitors. The rules are necessary in order to indicate the rights of the competing individuals; they are an expression of the structure of society and are designed to prevent any individual disrupting the structure and thereby spoiling life for his fellows.

In relation to oneself, sin expresses itself in *pride, self-sufficiency* and *self-centredness* (Mal. 4:1; Lk. 1:51; Jas. 4:6; 1 Jn. 2:16). It is the attitude of the person who not only puts himself first, but also resents any interference from outside in the running of his life. He is unconcerned about anybody except himself and his own pleasures, and he feels no need of the counsel or help of God in managing his own affairs. He thinks that he can do without God.

Sin thus affects every relationship of man, and its influence can be seen in every part of life; its badness corrupts his thoughts, sayings and deeds. The old-fashioned term for this pervasive effect of sin is 'total depravity'. But this must not be misunderstood. It is not to be denied that one person differs from another in degrees of goodness and evil. Even when measured by such an inadequate, external standard as the secular law, men manifestly differ considerably from one another. Nor should the existence of good deeds even in the worst of men be forgotten. The tendency of Christians is to deny that non-Christians can be good in any sense at all without the help of Christ. This is palpably false. Otherwise, all our moral comparisons between people would be nonsensical. The point is rather that none of us is free from the taint of sin; all of us are sufferers from a disease which affects the whole of our lives to different degrees, and none of us can cure himself. We cannot weigh our good deeds over against our evil deeds and claim that the former should be regarded as cancelling out the latter.

The fact that we are all sinners does not mean that we have lost the image of God. The Bible never suggests that sin leads to the loss of man's essential nature and destiny. Rather, we cease to reflect the character of God as fully as we should. If man was originally created good, we can say that we have lost that goodness, and indeed the Bible is unsparing in its delineation of the sheer wickedness of the human heart (Gn. 8:21; Je. 17:9; Rom. 3:9–18). And this is the condition of all of us. The sin of Adam is repeated in the lives of all men. The evil tendency is there from birth (Ps. 51:5). Theologians refer to this as 'original sin', meaning that our sinfulness is something present in our lives from the start; we inherit a sinful disposition and we live in a sinful environment which nourishes it and tempts it into sinful action. We are born as self-centred individuals and our natural tendency is to think of ourselves and ignore the claims of God and other people. The purpose of our upbringing and education is to wean us away from self-centredness; in this way much can be and is done to fit us for life in society, but without changing our essential nature. Sin remains in our lives and produces its effects.

What, then, are the effects of sin? It should not be forgotten that the existence of evil has 'cosmic' effects, to which we have already alluded. In the Bible, natural calamities, hard and unproductive labour, disease and so on are all regarded as reflections of the fact that the universe as a whole, and not merely mankind, fails to fulfil the divinely intended pattern; it is a 'fallen world' in which we live (*cf.* Gn. 3:14–19; Rom. 8:19–22). But our concern here is with the effects of human sin.

First, it leads to *suffering*, both for the guilty and the innocent, for the sinner himself and those affected by his actions. Sin violates the divine pattern for life. It shatters man's fellowship with his neighbours, hardens the sinner's heart from showing love to others, and cuts him off from communion with God.

It brings its own unpleasant consequences in this life, quite apart from the final judgment of God (Rom. 1:18–32; 2:5; Gal. 6:7). One of the ugliest features of sin is that it affects not only the sinner, but also a host of other people who had no part in his particular sin.

Second, sin *enslaves* the sinner. It is not just a matter of isolated sinful thoughts and deeds. Sin is an evil force which takes control of a person's heart and will; it gains an even tighter hold upon him so that he is more and more incapable of doing the right and the good. At times he may be an unconscious and willing victim; at others he may cry out against the evil force which grips him like a cancer and will not leave go (Rom. 7:14–20).

Third, sin leads to *guilt* in the sight of God. The word 'guilt' is often used to mean simply the subjective feeling of shame which a person may or may not have after doing what is wrong. Psychologists can offer cures for guilt-feelings, and these have their value when a person has an irrational sense of guilt. But the theological use of 'guilt' is akin to the legal use. It is an objective status in the eyes of the law or of God. It is the state of having broken the law or rejected the will of God, and is real and indisputable, whether or not the person himself feels 'guilty' about what he has done. Guilt means liability to condemnation and punishment; the sinner stands condemned in the sight of God (Rom. 3:19; Jas. 2:10).

Thus, fourth, sin leads to *punishment*. In ordinary usage the word 'punishment' expresses a variety of elements. Punishment may be designed to *deter* evil-doers from crime, or it may be meant to *restrain* a particular criminal from further criminal acts, or it may include the attempt to *reform* the criminal by transforming his evil disposition into a better one, or it may combine these features. But it also may contain an element of *retribution*. This is seen in the fact that punishment is inflicted only on the guilty, while attempts to deter, restrain or reform criminals or likely criminals need not be confined to those

66

who have actually broken the law. Retribution means the up-holding of the law against those who would break it. A law would not be a law if it could be broken with impunity and no attempt made to enforce it. A penalty does not merely deter people from breaking the law again, nor does it merely act as a disincentive to people against a prospective act of dis-obedience: 'I shall not do x because if I do I shall have to pay a fine'. It entails the idea of making some kind of satisfaction for the broken law. On a more personal level, it corresponds to the feeling that if we have hurt or offended somebody we ought to do something to 'make up' for the injury.

The thought of punishment or penalty is thus a complex one, and the various elements mentioned enter into the way in which sin is said to lead to a penalty. The penalty is summed up as death, which is the cessation of the divine life in man. Through sin fellowship and contact with God are broken; the sinner fears God's presence (Gn. 3:8; Lk. 5:8; 1 Jn. 2:28); and he passes out of God's care into the power of sin (Rom. 1:24ff.). The sinner can be said to die spiritually while he is still alive physic-ally. Physical death itself is symbolic and part of this spiritual death (Gn. 2:16f.; Rom. 5:12ff.; 6:23). Finally, the sinner suffers total exclusion from the presence of God; this is spoken of as hell or the second death (Mt. 25:41; 2 Thes. 1:9; Rev. 20:11-15). In a very real sense sin brings its own consequences with it; by nature it is self-destructive and cuts men off from God as the source of life. Yet this process is not something automatic and impersonal; ultimately it takes place by the will of God who cannot do other than cast impenitent sinners out of his presence, but who longs to turn them from their sin to righteousness.

Thus the sinner is in a state of death even in this life (Eph. 2:1-5). He is in desperate need of rescue before his present unhappy state gives way to final condemnation. How is rescue possible? Our attention is naturally drawn to the second Adam who 'to the fight and to the rescue came'. We must now look at the new creation in which God undoes the effects of sin in the present world through Jesus Christ.

Questions for study and discussion

1. *Does the Christian revelation place a question mark against any particular scientific theories of the origin of the universe and of mankind?*

2. *Discuss what is meant by the biblical teaching that man is made in the image of God. Do men still retain that image?*

3. *'Around the explanation of these three passages (Psalm 8:3f.; Job. 7:17f.; Hebrews 2:6–9), so closely linked, might be gathered no small part of the Biblical doctrine of man' (H. W. Robinson): discuss the question 'What is man?' in the light of these passages.*

4. *An old Jewish book states: 'Each of us has been the Adam of his own soul'. Discuss this statement in relation to the teaching of Paul in Romans 5:12–21.*

5. *'The common notion that sin is selfishness betrays a false assessment of its nature and gravity' (J. Murray): what, then, is the biblical view of the essence of sin?*

5

The person and work of Jesus

The central theme of Christian theology, that which gives it its *Christian* character, is the coming of Jesus into the world as its Saviour from sin (Mk. 10:45; Jn. 3:16; Tit. 2:11). His coming is both a revelation of the character of God as holy love and also the supreme act of love by which God reconciles sinful men to himself (2 Cor. 5:19).

Jesus Christ as God and man
(John 1:1–18; Philippians 2:5–11)

We have already seen how Jesus is described in the New Testament as the Son of God and the Lord, and there is no need to repeat the evidence here. At the same time he is described, often quite unconsciously, as a real human being. He had a human mother (Gal. 4:4), and he grew up like any other boy to manhood (Lk. 2:40, 52). He experienced the emotions and feelings common to all men – love (Mk. 10:21), sorrow (Jn. 11:33–36), anger (Mk. 3:5; 10:14) and compassion (Mk. 6:34). The experiences of hunger, thirst and sheer weariness were real ones for him (Jn. 4:6ff.; 19:28). Although he had prophetic insights and knowledge not shared by other men, he also had a genuinely human mind and needed to ask questions to obtain information of which he was ignorant (Mk. 9:21; 11:13). He felt the need to pray (Mk. 1:35; 6:46; Heb. 5:7). He was made in the likeness of sinful mankind (Rom. 8:3), and

69

so he knew what it was like to be tempted beyond measure (Mk. 1:13; 14:32ff.; Heb. 2:18), but, unlike all other men, he never yielded to temptation (Mt. 4:1–11; Jn. 8:46; 2 Cor. 5:21; Heb. 4:15; 1 Pet. 2:22). In short, the Jesus who is presented in the New Testament as the Son of God also appears as a perfectly real man.

We naturally look for some explanation of this paradox. What was the purpose of God in bringing his Son into the world in this way? To put the question in this way directs us to an examination of what Jesus did. We may, in other words, make some progress in understanding the kind of *person* that he was by looking at the *task* which he came to do. This task was to be the Saviour of men. In order to be a Saviour, it was necessary for Jesus to be both God and man. Otherwise his work would have been incomplete and unable to meet the deepest needs of sinners.

It was necessary, then, for Jesus to be truly God. It needed the advent of God himself among men to show clearly the greatness of his saving love by which he wins and woos men back to himself. For a lover to send somebody other than himself to convey a message of love suggests that he is not prepared to involve himself fully in demonstrating his love. The greatness of God's love is seen in that he came himself in the person of Jesus. The Father was prepared to give his only Son as the demonstration of his love; Jews who knew the story of how Abraham was prepared to sacrifice his son, Isaac, would not be slow to grasp the point (Jn. 1:14–18; Gn. 22:2; Jn. 3:16; 1 Jn. 4:9f.).

More is involved, however, than a demonstration of love. The coming of Jesus demonstrates the involvement of God to the full in bearing human sin and himself enduring its consequences (2 Cor. 5:19). Indeed, only God himself could deal with the problem of sin by bearing the cost of forgiveness himself. It is relatively easy for me to pardon someone who has hurt me and then does his best to make amends to me; that costs me very little (beyond the willingness to change my mind – which is hard for proud people), but it does not give any assurance to the offender that I may not change my attitude back from friendship to anger. It is much more costly for me to bear the brunt of somebody else's offence against me and demonstrate my willingness to forgive. Only such willingness can provide forgiveness where the offender remains at first recalcitrant; and only such willingness can make it plain that the forgiveness is genuine and irrevocable. Our assurance of forgiveness from God rests on the fact that God was in Christ reconciling the world to himself.

At the same time, it is important to be clear that it was necessary for Jesus to be truly man. The other side of the picture is that Jesus stands before God on behalf of men, bears the judgment upon their sins, and intercedes for them. Only a man could identify himself with other men and take their place in making a perfect offering to God (Heb. 2:14–18). Paul makes a comparison between the evil brought upon the human race by the first man, Adam, and the blessing brought by the second man, the last Adam, who became the representative of his fellow men and atoned for their sins (Rom. 5:12–21; 1 Cor. 15:21f.). Through this man sinners can approach God and find peace with him (Heb. 4:14 – 5:10). The coming of Jesus as a human being demonstrates that God's salvation is for the human race.

These considerations show that for the sake of our salvation it was necessary that the Saviour should be both God and man. But now we must ask how this was possible. Again, as was the case in attempting to explain the nature of God as three Persons in one, we find ourselves up against the barrier caused by human finite thinking and the limitations of human language. We are trying to explain how one person can be both Creator and created, how one person can share the apparently contradictory properties of being human and divine. It is safe to say that an explanation of this mystery is in principle impossible for us.

We cannot describe how it is possible. What we can do is to see why various explanations that have from time to time been offered are inadequate. By ruling out various misleading explanations, we may come a stage nearer to stating the mystery adequately, even if we cannot explain it for ourselves.

A number of early Christians, for example, solved the problem by stating that Jesus was a divine being who only appeared to be human for a short time and then changed back to his divine nature. (This view was called Docetism, from a Latin verb meaning 'to seem'.) We can easily see that this view will not do, for it denies that Jesus was a real man, and thus prevents him from truly identifying with the human race. There are still people today who would formally reject this view, but in effect hold to it by playing down the fact that Jesus was really a man who could feel tired and hungry. Another view was that Jesus was a man all right, but he was not divine in nature; rather God chose him because of his faultless life and adopted him as his son. This view obviously falls into the opposite error of denying that Jesus was truly divine, to say nothing of its misinterpretation of the clear teaching of the New Testament. Other views agree that Jesus was both human and divine, but fall into error by making him a sort of semi-human, semi-divine being, partly one and partly the other. Still others suggest that Jesus had two separate natures, one human and the other divine, almost like a Jekyll-and-Hyde case of dual identity. The truth is that we cannot put into words how a person can be both fully divine and fully human; we have no analogies by which to explain it. Rather we have to hold fast to the biblical teaching that the Son of God became a man without ceasing to be the Son of God (Jn. 1:14; 2 Cor. 8:9; Phil. 2:5-11).

Clearly this poses problems. We have seen that God is all-knowing, all-powerful and all-present. How, then, could God become incarnate in man who possesses none of these features? One popular theory speaks of the Son of God emptying himself

(Greek *kenōsis*) of his divine attributes in order to become man, while retaining his love and moral perfection. Clearly there is some truth in this theory. In Philippians 2:6–8 we are told that though he was originally in the form of God, Jesus took a human form. He certainly gave up the outward, visible glory of the Godhead in order to appear in the humble form of a man. When, however, it is suggested that Jesus had no more than the fallible knowledge of an ordinary man, or that he had no super-natural powers whatever, we are bound to protest that the Gospels present him otherwise and that views of this kind destroy any continuity between the pre-incarnate Son of God and the incarnate one. The truth is rather that by means of some exercise of the attributes of God, Jesus was able to appear as a real man, and yet as more than a man.

If Jesus was the Son of God, we need not be surprised if both his entry into the world and his departure from it were not like those of other men. The New Testament is reticent on both points. Although it records the fact of the resurrection and tells how Jesus was seen by his followers after he had returned to life, it records no eye-witness account of the actual moment of resurrection. Similarly, it says little about the manner of Jesus' birth. Apart from the birth narratives, there is just sufficient evidence to indicate that the New Testament writers were not ignorant that his birth was unusual (*cf.* Jn. 1:13; 6:42; 8:41f.; Gal. 4:4). This silence is readily understandable, especially during the lifetime of Mary.

According to the birth narratives, the birth of Jesus was the result not of normal human conception by the action of Mary's husband, but of the special operation of the Holy Spirit (Lk. 1:34f.). This is sheer miracle, but it imposes no greater strain on faith than the miracle of the incarnation itself. It is sometimes objected that if Jesus was born of a virgin, he is not in every respect like us (*cf.* Heb. 2:17). But the objection is an empty one, since the manner of his conception did not affect the reality of his subsequent human life and experience. Nor are

73

the alternative theories any better. Either he was the illegitimate son of Mary (as Jewish slander asserted; *cf*. Jn. 8:41) or he was the natural son of Joseph and Mary. Both suggestions run counter to the New Testament evidence, and fail to do justice to the mystery of the person of Jesus. What the Bible stresses is not so much the virginity of Mary as the positive action of the Spirit, but these are inseparable.

The ministry of Jesus (Mark 1: 14–45; Luke 4:14–30)

In the Apostles' Creed there is a sudden jump from 'Born of the Virgin Mary' to 'Suffered under Pontius Pilate'. We might be tempted to draw the false inference that what happened in between these two terminal events in the life of Jesus is unimportant for Christian belief. It is, however, being increasingly recognized that the theology of the early church developed out of what Jesus did and taught during his ministry. A theology that ignores the contents of the Gospels is one-sided and defective. We can sum up the presentation of Jesus in the Gospels in some five aspects.

First, Jesus came to proclaim the *Kingship of God*. He came to a world that was under the sway of Satan (Lk. 4:5–7; Jn. 12:31) and brought to it the message that God had now begun to act in a new way to establish his own reign of righteousness and salvation (Mk. 1:14f.; Lk. 9:48; 16:13). It was time for men to be released from the power of Satan (Lk. 13:16) and the demons. Let them follow the teaching of Jesus and become his disciples (Mk. 1:16–20; 10:14; Lk. 6:46ff.). Those who responded to Jesus' call were taught the new way of life associated with the rule of God (Mt. 5–7) and were sent out to spread further the good news that God's rule was beginning (Mk. 3:13–15; 5:19; Mt. 28:16–20). Jesus was the prophet divinely authorized to announce what was happening.

Second, Jesus was more than merely a prophet of what God was doing. His preaching fulfilled the Old Testament proph-

74

ecies of the coming of one who would usher in the kingdom of God (Lk. 4:18–21). He was himself the *Messiah* (*i.e.* an anointed king) through whom God was exercising his saving rule (Lk. 1:68–79). Pilate got the message, as he showed by placing the words 'The King of the Jews' on the cross (Jn. 19:19–22) – although his understanding was superficial. Jesus himself, however, refrained from open use of the title, probably because of the misleading associations it could have had for Jews who thought of the coming of a nationalist, military leader. Jesus was prepared to be addressed as 'Son of David' (Mk. 10:47f.; 11:9f.; 12:35–37), a title which was tantamount to 'Messiah', but his own preference was for 'Son of man'. This phrase, which simply means 'the Man' in Hebrew idiom, is found in Daniel 7, where it refers to the representative of the saints of God who, after their defeat by their enemies, receive power and dominion from God. By adopting this title, Jesus was in effect claiming to be the true Representative and Leader of God's people. Although his authority was rejected by men and he would be put to death, he would be vindicated by God (Mk. 8:31, 38; 13:24–27; 14:62; Lk. 17:24f.); at the last judgment the decisive factor would be the attitude of men to the Son of man and his corresponding acceptance or rejection of them (Mt. 25:31ff.; Mk. 8:38; Lk. 12:8f.).

Third, Jesus understood his task as the Son of man in the light of another Old Testament figure. This was the *suffering Servant of God* described in Isaiah 40–53. Here the Servant is at first a symbol for the people of Israel, or rather for the pious core of the people, who were chosen by God to establish justice in the earth and to bring salvation to men (Is. 42:1–7). As the prophecy progresses, however, and the prophet became increasingly concious of the sin and inadequacy of Israel, he was led to look beyond the nation to an individual servant who would take on the role intended for Israel and would perfectly fulfil the purpose of God by his own suffering (Is. 52:13–53:12). Jesus recognized this role as the one that he was called to fulfil

(Mt. 12:18–21; Mk. 10:45; Lk. 22:24–27, 37; 1 Pet. 2:21–24).

Fourth, Jesus saw his task as more than the proclamation of a message. His aim was to be the *Deliverer of men and women* from the bonds of sin and evil, and this required action as well as words. At the outset of his ministry he associated himself with the sinners whom he came to save by submitting to John's baptism (Mt. 3:13–17; *cf.* Mk. 10:38f.; Lk. 12:50), and in his death he paid the ransom by which men are released from the power and guilt of sin and enabled to enter the kingdom of God (Mk. 10:45; 14:22–24; Jn. 10:11, 17; 12:32). His death was the culmination of a ministry in which he brought healing to the sick, release to the demon-possessed, love and hope to the despised and lonely, and moral challenge to the sinful. Such a task brought him into constant conflict with those who sided with the forces of evil (Mt. 4:1–11; Mk. 2:1 – 3:6; 11:27 – 12:40; Lk. 11:20). The final show-down brought him to the cross and apparent defeat – but in reality to vindication by God and the defeat of evil (Jn. 12:31–33).

So, fifth, we can see in the ministry of Jesus the *revelation of God* in both his love which gives to the uttermost in order to save sinners (Mk. 2:15–17; Lk. 15:1–10) and his judgment against all hypocrisy and sin (Mt. 23). As the one who loved sinners but warned against their sin, Jesus called men to accept the rule of God with all its blessings and obligations. His coming created a crisis in which men had to decide for or against God, and none could remain unmoved or neutral; 'He who is not with me is against me' (Lk. 11:23).

The death and resurrection of Jesus (Luke 22–24)

Nobody can read the story of the death of Jesus without realizing that it was remarkably unlike the death of any other man and that it demands some sort of explanation. It was, of course, one of the most cruel and painful forms of death that can be imagined, and contemporary authors spoke of crucifixion with horror in their voices. It was not this, however, that made the death of Jesus unique. Hundreds of other people, perhaps thousands, underwent the same horrible torture, and their fate has been illustrated by the discovery in 1968 of the skeleton of a young man who had been crucified in first-century Palestine. This was the normal fate of rebels and rebellious slaves. Jesus, however, was plainly declared to be innocent of any crime by the Roman governor who examined him (Lk. 23:13–16). He was put to death on the charge of being 'The King of the Jews', but it was the Jews who instigated his death and bent justice to achieve their end. Jesus himself met his death willingly, choosing not to flee from it. Indeed he probably precipitated it by voluntarily going up to Jerusalem. Yet the thought of his death caused him tremendous agony of soul, and he longed that he might not have to face it (Mk. 14:36).

After his death his disciples made the most remarkable claims about him. They asserted that he was the crucified Messiah or king of the Jews, an idea that was completely inconceivable to people who had expected a victorious king, and well calculated to alienate support for the new religion centred on Jesus (1 Cor. 1:23; 'Christ' is a Greek word meaning the same as Hebrew 'Messiah', *i.e.* 'anointed (king)'). The disciples of Jesus also argued that although wicked men had put him to death, it was really due to the deliberate plan of God, who brought it about (Acts 2:23). They said that after his death Jesus had reappeared to them, and that all this showed him to be none other than the Son of God (Gal. 2:20).

We may find a clue to the meaning of this most unusual death in the remarkable cry of the crucified man: 'My God, my God, why hast thou forsaken me?' (Mk.15:34, quoting Ps. 22:1). The most probable explanation of these words is that Jesus felt himself to be abandoned by God whom he usually address-ed in the most intimate manner possible as 'Father'. There would seem to be only one adequate explanation of this exper-ience. Jesus, who by his own free choice was 'reckoned with transgressors' (Lk. 22:37), was at that point so closely identified with sinners through bearing the burden of their sin that he felt to the full that exclusion from fellowship with God and from the help of God which is the inevitable consequence of sin (*cf.* Gal. 3:13). The unanimous witness of the New Testament is that what Jesus did on the cross was done for us; because of what he endured we need never suffer that exclusion from the presence of God which is the result and penalty of sin. Only one word is really adequate to describe this role of Jesus on the cross, the word 'substitute' which means that because Jesus in his love has suffered on our behalf we need never suffer the penalty of our sins.

The story of what God has done for sinful men does not end with the cross. There still remains his mighty act in which he set his seal on the work of his Son, the resurrection. The resurrection is to be understood as a historical event in the same sense as the death of Jesus was a historical event. That is to say, it really happened, even if nobody actually saw Jesus rise from the dead and only a comparatively small number of people saw him alive after his death. Both events are, to be sure, more than merely 'historical'. In each case the subject was the Son of God, and each act had spiritual effects. But the point to be stressed is that the resurrection was 'historical' in the sense that something actually happened in this world which affected other events, even if it is impossible to prove to the most hardened sceptic that it happened. What must be denied is that the resurrection of Jesus was merely a conviction in the minds of the disciples, with no basis in history.

Our concern here is with the significance of this event. It was a proof of God's justice in that the innocent suffering of Jesus was not allowed to take place without the vindication of Jesus as innocent. The Christian can be confident that God who raised Jesus from the dead is the moral Sovereign of the universe; that he will also vindicate every righteous sufferer who trusts in him and will bring him into his presence (2 Cor. 4:14). The resurrection is also the proof that God accepted the death of Jesus on the cross as a full and adequate means of salvation for all mankind (Acts 2:32–36). At the same time, the resurrection showed that the power of death, both physical and spiritual, is not final, since God can raise up the dead to a new life beyond the grave. The resurrection of Jesus is the first-fruits or precursor of the resurrection of believers (1 Cor. 15:23). Thus, the resurrection is the sign of Christ's victory over sin and death and the guarantee of life for his people.

Forty days after the resurrection Jesus was seen by his disciples for the last time, and before their eyes he ascended into heaven. There was to be one exceptional reappearance of Jesus to Saul of Tarsus at a later point (Acts 1:1–11; 9:1–22). The ascension thus marked the departure of Jesus as a visible being from the earth until the day when he will return in the same way as he departed (Acts 1:11; Rev. 1:7). Yet he is not spiritually 'absent'. Another Comforter, the invisible Spirit of Christ, takes his place, so that in a very real sense he is still with his people and will remain with them until the end of the world (Mt. 28:20; Jn. 14:16, 18). Until that day Jesus is said, in the symbolical language of Psalm 110:1, to be sitting at the right hand of God the Father (Heb. 1:13). He has entered heaven as a man (Heb. 4:14–16), and the significance of his sitting beside God is that he has finished his sacrificial work and obtained an eternal salvation for men (Heb. 10:12–14). All that remains is that he waits for the final overthrow of evil (1 Cor. 15:25; Heb. 1:13).

The need for the cross (Ephesians 2:1–16)

So far we have been merely indicating the facts about the work of Jesus, although it has been impossible to do so without already making use of theological terms. Now we must consider in greater detail the theological significance of the events recorded in the Gospels, and for this purpose we must make particular use of the doctrinal commentary provided by the Epistles.

We have already seen that all men are regarded as sinners in the sight of God. They have chosen to obey sin instead of God, and in consequence of this they stand under his judgment. They have entered into a bondage from which they can find no release, and they are liable to death as the penalty of their sin.

In this situation three problems can be said to arise. How can God win men back from love of sin to love of himself? How can he forgive sinners without condoning their sin or denying his own implacable opposition to it? And how can he free men from sin so that they may become his willing servants? It is important to recognize that these are, as it were, problems for God. Some writers give the impression that the difficulties are all on man's side. Conscious of his sin, he has neither the desire nor the ability to return to God, and he fears that if he does try to return he will not be accepted by him. But this is only half the story. In a very real sense, God has the difficulty that he cannot condone sin and yet he longs to restore sinful man to his favour. It is at the cross that all the barriers between God and man are broken down. It becomes possible for God to forgive sin, and so a path is opened up for man to return to God.

The cross shows God's love (1 John 4:7–12)

The New Testament writers emphasize that the restoration of peace between God and sinners has its source in the love of God the Father. Sometimes theologians have given the impression that Jesus had to placate an angry God and wrest forgiveness out of an unwilling Judge; some basis for such views might be found in those places where Jesus is said to intercede for us with the Father (Rom. 8:34; 1 Jn. 2:1). But this is to misunderstand these passages and to press the metaphor of intercession beyond its intended limit. Nowhere is it ever suggested that the Father is unwilling to respond to the work of the Son on our behalf. On the contrary, it was because the Father so loved the world that he gave his Son to die for us (Jn. 3:16). In the cross, God the Father demonstrates his love to us (Rom. 5:8). He did not spare his Son but freely gave him up for us all (Rom. 8:32; *cf.* Eph. 2:7; Tit. 3:4; 1 Pet. 1:3; 1 Jn. 4:9f.). It was the Father whose love initiated the act of reconciliation between himself and sinners.

Consequently, the cross must be seen as God's tender appeal to us to return to him and abandon our sin. It is a demonstration of his love for sinners. And this love extends to all sinners. It is universal in its intent, even if not all men respond to its appeal: the grace of God has appeared for the salvation of *all* men (Tit. 2:11). Some thinkers have urged that when we have said this, we have said all that can be said. A demonstration of God's love is held to be an adequate means of reconciliation or atonement between him and sinners. But this is far from being the truth. For it is a sad fact of experience that a mere demonstration of love cannot break the power of evil or wipe out the guilt of sin. The love of parents for a rebellious son who has embarked on a career of crime may make him want to give up his evil ways, but it cannot break the stranglehold of avarice in his heart, nor can it wipe out the crime that he has already committed. For the love of God seen in the cross to have any effect, it must be *redemptive* love. The cross shows us love in action, God actually doing something to provide our salvation, and only because it is that kind of love has it the power to win us back to God.

The cross as a sacrificial offering (Hebrews 9)

In the Old Testament legislation it was provided that sinners could make an offering to God as a means of securing pardon for their sins. There were various different forms of sacrifice for different purposes. Sometimes a sacrifice was simply a means of expressing thanks to God or a sign of communion between the worshippers and God, but certain sacrifices were specifically made to deal with the guilt caused by sin. The idea was that the sinner confessed his sins to God and offered a sacrificial animal to God, who accepted its death, as symbolized by the shedding of its blood, as an atoning offering for sin (Lv. 17:11; Heb. 9:22). God accepted the death of the animal instead of the death of the sinner as an offering for sin, always provided that the sinner was using the offering to express his repentance.

The New Testament takes over the sacrificial language of the Old and uses it to express in bold metaphor the significance of the death of Jesus. The sacrificial term 'blood' is used more often than any other expression to indicate the death of Jesus (Mk. 14:24; Jn. 6:53–56; Acts 20:28; Rom. 3:25; 5:9; Col. 1:20; Heb. 9:14; 13:11f.; 1 Jn. 1:7; Rev. 1:5). This is all the more remarkable when we recall that death by crucifixion did not involve the shedding of blood to any significant extent. Again, Jesus is called the Lamb of God (Jn. 1:29; 1 Pet. 1:19; Rev. 5:6), and his death is described as a sacrificial offering to God (Eph. 5:2; Heb. 10:5ff.). Not only so, but when the New Testament writers look back at the Old Testament in the light of the death of Jesus, they affirm that the old sacrifices were not efficacious in themselves – how could the blood of bulls or goats take away sin (Heb. 10:4)? Rather they were simply God-given pictures or 'types' which provided the imagery with which to understand the 'real' sacrifice, that of Jesus. It was the latter which gave them their efficacy since they were really meant to be pointers to it (Heb. 9:9–14; 10:1–4). The cross, therefore, is to be seen as an act in time with eternal consequences, so that God could forgive sins committed both before and after it.

The word 'sacrifice' has lost its biblical meaning in popular parlance. Today it simply means the giving up of something precious, often for the sake of somebody else. A man who rescues somebody from a burning house at the cost of his own life can be said to have sacrificed his own life. This fact reminds us that sacrifice is costly. The worshipper had to surrender something valuable when he made his offering; the cost of God's sacrifice was that he gave up his own Son to the suffering involved in the cross. But this idea of cost is only part of the concept. A sacrifice is also something done for the benefit of somebody else (or for the good of some cause). It is only if I am trying to save somebody from a burning house that my death in it becomes a sacrifice: otherwise it may be nothing more than a tragic accident. The point of the animal sacrifice in the Old Testament was that it was for the good of the worshipper and saved him from having to die for his sins. But the biblical use of the term goes further still, and here it parts company from the modern use of the word: a sacrifice is a costly offering on behalf of somebody else *made to God*. It is something that is offered to God in order to deal with sin. It can be regarded as a gift to God to make up for a fault, but, at a deeper level, it is the bearing of the penalty due to sin to save the sinner from bearing that penalty himself.

That is what Jesus has done for us. He died the death which is the result and penalty of sin, and so he has released us from the need to die that death. He has provided the means by which sin is 'covered' and the wrath of God is 'propitiated' or appeased. So fellowship is restored between God and men (Rom. 3:25; Heb. 10:19f.; 1 Jn. 2:2). To describe this act of Jesus we need to use the words 'penal substitution', which convey the truth that Jesus has endured the consequences of sin on behalf of mankind. Consequently, when a sinner comes to God, identifying himself with Jesus in submission to the divine judgment on sin, and trusting him as his Saviour, he finds that he has nothing to contribute of his own, for Jesus has done all that was necessary, and that he is pardoned by the God against whom he had sinned.

The cross as deliverance from sin (Revelation 5:1–14)

The concept of sacrifice is the most important image used in the New Testament to express the meaning of the death of Jesus, for it brings out the significance of the cross in restoring the sinner to a right relation with God. But when we consider the relation of the sinner to sin, the concepts of victory and redemption become important.

The ministry of Jesus can be regarded as a continuous conflict with the power of Satan who sought to deflect Jesus from his path at the beginning (Mt. 4:1–9) and continued to oppose him throughout its course. The death of Jesus represents the high point in that conflict. It can be regarded as the attempt of evil men, inspired by Satan (*cf.* Lk. 22:3), to put an end to what Jesus was doing by killing him. But it turned out to be a complete failure, for Jesus rose from the dead, and his work still continues. Satan could not tempt Jesus to sin during his ministry, nor could he make him yield to the power of death. Rather it was Satan who was judged and defeated at the cross, so that now he ranks as a conquered foe whose final doom is sealed. Like a mortally wounded animal, he continues to struggle, but his death is only a matter of time (Jn. 12:31). He and his minions can no longer lord it over those who trust in Christ, for Jesus Christ is now enthroned as Lord (Eph. 1:20f.; Phil. 2:9–11; Heb. 2:14f.; 1 Pet. 3:22).

With this thought of victory over Satan is connected the imagery of redemption, the setting free of those who were once the captives of Satan and sin. Again the picture is an Old Testament one, drawn from the use of the word to describe God's mighty act of delivering his people from bondage in Egypt. The tremendous cost of the operation is the point of emphasis, rather than the idea that God has to stoop to pay anybody to set his people free (Ex. 6:6; Ne. 1:10; Pss. 77:14f.; 130:8; Is. 43:1–4; 63:9; Je. 50:34). The death of Jesus is depicted as the culminating act of divine deliverance (Lk. 1:68; 24:21; Tit. 2:14). At the same time the picture probably reflects the legal ceremony in which a slave was set free from his old master by the payment of a ransom price (1 Cor. 6:20; 7:23). The death of Jesus is the cost paid by God to deliver men from sin (Eph. 1:7; 1 Pet. 1:18), so that they may now become his willing servants (1 Cor. 7:22f.); they look forward to the day when Satan is finally overcome and they can enter into the joy of full redemption (Lk. 21:28; Rom. 8:23; Eph. 4:30).

Questions for study and discussion

1. *Would anything have been lost from the Christian religion if Jesus had not been a real man?*

2. *'Perfect humanity is divinity' : is it?*

3. *What evidence can be gathered from the first three Gospels to show that entry to the kingdom of God depends upon a person's attitude to Jesus? (A concordance will be found useful here.)*

4. *'If Christ had done less than die for us, there would have been no atonement' (J. Denney) : why not?*

5. *How would you get across the significance of the death of Jesus to modern people who are not familiar with such ideas as sacrifice and redemption, and think that they are out of date?*

6

The life of the Christian

We have now looked at God's original intention for the world
and the way in which mankind has fallen into sin and rebellion
against God's plan. We have seen how Jesus Christ came to be
the Saviour of men. The next stage in the study of Christian
doctrine is to consider the new life which God bestows upon
those who accept Jesus as their Saviour from sin. We shall begin
by looking at two general words which are used to describe our
experience as Christians; then we shall discuss four different
aspects of the Christian life; and finally we shall consider the
nature of our response to God's gift of salvation and eternal life.

Salvation (1 Peter 1:3–12)

The first of the two general terms used in the Bible for the great
gift which men receive as a result of the work of Christ is
salvation (Rom. 1:16). It is an interesting fact that the corresponding verb 'to be saved' is used in all three tenses. Christians are
people who *have been* saved: the time when they put their trust
in Jesus marks the beginning of their experience of salvation
(Eph. 2:5, 8). They are people who daily *are being* saved as they
continually experience more and more of the love of Christ and
the power of the Spirit and increase in faith and knowledge
(2 Cor. 2:15; *cf*. Eph. 3:14ff.). But their salvation is not yet
fully given to them, and the Bible also speaks of it as a future
gift: they *will be* saved in the day of God's final triumph (2 Tim.

4:18), and so their present life is one of hope for that full, future salvation (Rom. 8:24). We find that these three tenses of salvation are placed alongside one another in 1 Peter 1:3-5. They point to the fact that Christians believe in one who is able to save 'now and always' (Heb. 7:25 TEV) those who come to God by him. His name 'Jesus' portrays his character as the 'Saviour'.

The completeness and sufficiency of God's gift is seen not only in the fact that it embraces past, present and future, but also in the fact that it is both negative and positive in its effects. Negatively, it is salvation *from* sin and the wrath of God (1 Tim. 1:15; Rom. 5:9): to 'save' is in effect to 'rescue' or 'deliver' men from an unpleasant fate. Positively, salvation brings us into a knowledge of God (1 Tim. 2:4).

From first to last, salvation is the gift of God to us in Jesus Christ (Acts 15:11). It was God who chose to prepare a saved people for himself (Eph. 1:3-6). He acted by his Spirit to communicate the good news of salvation to us and to awaken the possibility of faith in our hearts (1 Thes. 1:4-6). And it is God who continues to keep us by his power and who will bring us at last into the full enjoyment of salvation (1 Pet. 1:5; the whole process is summarized in Rom. 8:29f.).

Eternal life (John 6:27–71)

The word 'salvation' conveys the idea of rescue from danger and the restoration of peace and well-being. The thought of 'eternal life' suggests the resurrection of the dead. Sinners can properly be regarded as dead to the spiritual life of God while they are in this world, and they stand under condemnation to eternal death in the next world (Rom. 6:23; Eph. 2:1-5). The coming of Jesus has brought the possibility of true life to them (2 Tim. 1:10). This means that for the Christian physical death is not the termination of real life, but is the gateway to everlasting life in the presence of God and of Christ (Jn. 5:29;

11:23). Such life is 'eternal' not merely in the sense that it is everlasting, but also and above all in the sense that it is the life of the eternal God shared with his creatures (Jn. 5:25f.; 2 Cor. 4:10f.).

Eternal life can in fact be defined as the experience of knowing God (Jn. 17:3) – an experience which is unknown to the sinner (Eph. 4:17f.). But although it is often thought that eternal life simply means the future life of heaven after death, it is in fact the *present* possession of every Christian here and now in this world (Jn. 5:24; 6:47). Our present life as Christians is a foretaste of the life of heaven. Here and now we can know God and experience his love (Jn. 11:25f.; 1 Tim. 4:8; 1 Jn. 3:14; 5:11). Even though our outward bodies perish, our 'inner man' possesses an indestructible life from God (2 Cor. 4:16), and in the end we shall openly possess that life which is now our hidden possession (Col. 3:3f.). Our present experience of eternal life is, therefore, incomplete and 'hidden'; it depends on our continual sustenance with the bread of life (Jn. 6:35, 54). One day it will blossom forth into the full experience of being in the presence of God.

Peace with God (Ephesians 2:11–18)

In attempting to define more closely the nature of the salvation and eternal life which we enjoy as Christians, we shall make use of four key concepts. The first of these is *peace*, and we shall explain it by means of a further three significant words.

Paul uses the word *justification* as a technical term for the gracious act of God in pardoning sinners and restoring them to a right relationship with himself. This is a word drawn from legal terminology. It brings before our eyes the picture of a judge who declares the man in the dock to be innocent of the charges brought against him. In the Old Testament there are strict warnings to judges that they must not justify, *i.e.* acquit, evil, guilty men (Pr. 17:15). In the New Testament, however,

88

we find that God himself acquits sinful, ungodly men (Rom. 5:8f.). How can this be?

It is possible only because in his grace and love God gave his Son to be the sacrifice for our sin (Rom. 3:24f.). He came into this world and lived a life of perfect obedience to God. He identified himself with sinners and their sin, and on their behalf and in their place he submitted to the just claims of God's law and bore its curse (2 Cor. 5:21; Gal. 3:13). It is because he bore our condemnation and offered a perfectly righteous life to God that God is able to acquit those who make themselves one with Jesus. God regards them as righteous not because of anything that they have done to deserve it, but simply because they trust in Christ alone as their righteousness (Rom. 4:20–25; 1 Cor. 1:30). Those who admit their sinfulness before God and put their trust in Christ no longer receive the reward due to their sin, but are freely acquitted or justified by God for the sake of Christ.

Because of what Christ has done, sinners no longer need to try to do good works as a means of pleasing God and winning salvation (Rom. 4:5; Eph. 2:8–10). Indeed any such attempt is ruled out of court by what God has done for them; it would be an insult to God's love and to the perfection of Christ's sacrifice if we felt that we needed to do something else in order to get right with God. Nevertheless, true faith in God will inevitably express itself in good works; there is all the difference in the world between trying to win God's favour by establishing our own goodness and showing our gratitude to him for what he has done for us by expressing our faith and love in action. Good works are the necessary *fruit* of justification, but they are not its *cause*.

Justification is a legal word, and it is used almost exclusively by Paul. Another, perhaps more easily understood, word which conveys essentially the same meaning is *forgiveness*. This word takes us into the realm of personal relationships (Rom. 4:7; Lk. 7:36–50). It is used to describe the effects of Jesus' death on the cross (Mt. 26:28; Eph. 1:7), and Jesus himself declared God's forgiveness to sinners (Lk. 7:48). The way to forgiveness is through faith in him (Acts 10:43).

Forgiveness occurs when someone whom we have offended or hurt agrees to forget what we have done and not to hold it against us. Such an act may be very costly to the person who forgives. In the human situation this may be because of the very real loss that he has suffered, for example, if somebody has murdered a member of his family. But it may also be hard for men to swallow their hurt pride and forgive what is in reality a small insult. In the case of God it is obvious that there can be no false pride to be overcome. Nevertheless, it was costly for God to forgive, since the effect of human sin was to disrupt the creation which he had made as something good and beautiful. God forgives by taking upon himself the hurt done by man and absorbing it in his love, and this we see happening in the cross when the Son of God suffered patiently the rejection and cruelty of men, without retaliation.

At the same time there is another side to forgiveness. The offender can receive forgiveness only when he is penitent and sorry for what he has done. But this is something that men are scarcely capable of. In Jesus Christ, however, we see man's perfect representative offering himself to God on our behalf and doing for us what we could not do for ourselves. It is as we identify ourselves with him that God's forgiveness becomes a reality for us.

Justification is an act of God as the sovereign Judge. Forgiveness, however, can be performed by men. Those who receive free and unmerited divine forgiveness must be ready to forgive others (Mt. 6:14f.; Eph. 4:32). Indeed, if they are not ready to forgive other people, God will not forgive their sins. While justification is usually regarded as a single act of God (anticipating his verdict on the day of judgment), forgiveness is something for which we need to pray daily (Mt. 6:12; 1 Jn. 1:9), for although justified, we are still prone to sin and need to seek forgiveness from God.

Justification and forgiveness are two of the terms which describe the process leading to peace between God and man. The third term for this process is *reconciliation*. This word presupposes the existence of a state of enmity between two people, so that they are not on friendly terms with each other. If I have an enemy, I may need to take the initiative by attempting to reconcile him to me. It is doubtless significant that in the New Testament God is never the object of reconciliation by men; they do not need to do anything to make him their friend, and in the light of what we have already learned about justification and forgiveness, this should not surprise us. Rather, God himself is the one who reconciles rebellious sinners to himself, and once again the means involved is the death of Jesus. By the death of Jesus, who bore our sins, God makes it plain that he does not hold our sins against us; there is no enmity on his side. He invites us to accept the reconciliation as an act already completed on his side (2 Cor. 5:18–20; Rom. 5:10f.). To put the point otherwise, Jesus can be represented as the mediator between God and man, who brings about reconciliation between the two parties separated by human sin (1 Tim. 2:5f.). Yet, as in the picture of Jesus interceding for us with God, there is no suggestion that God is an unwilling partner to the action of Jesus.

Reconciliation means the restoration of peace. Those who have been justified by faith enjoy peace with God (Rom. 5:1). They need no longer fear the wrath of God, but can now approach him with confidence. For peace is not simply a negative concept, the absence of enmity and war; positively it refers to the state of well-being which becomes possible when enmity has ceased.

It is true that those who have been restored to a right relationship with God may still sin against him and need forgiveness and cleansing. They are at one and the same time justified and yet still sinners; but because they trust in Christ they need not fear God's condemnation, although this is in no

sense a licence to sin. The person who goes on sinning deliberately shows that he has not truly understood the meaning
of forgiveness.

Sons of God (Matthew 6:24-34)

The new situation that has arisen through the work of Christ
and its acceptance by believers is peace. With it there comes a
new status for those who have been reconciled to God. They
are now reckoned as members of God's family and consequently as heirs who are qualified to receive the blessing which
he has promised to his children (Tit. 3:7).

The act whereby men enter into peace with God and become
his children is such a decisive one that it can be described as a
conversion (Mt. 18:1-4). The word itself means not so much a
transformation or alteration (as when a gas cooker is converted
to operate on a new type of fuel or an electronic device converts
one kind of current into another) as rather a change in direction.
It involves a 'right-about turn' in one's way of life. Concretely
it means turning from worship of idols to the worship of God,
from an old style of living with its sin to the new way of life in
which God is Lord and Master (1 Thes. 1:9f.). Men must be
ready for the humiliating step of becoming like helpless
children who cannot do anything for themselves but must trust in
the care of their parents. From a human point of view, becoming
a Christian involves an act of conversion in which we begin life
all over again and go in a different direction. In Matthew 18:1-4
Jesus is using the idea of becoming like children in a metaphorical way to signify going back to the beginning. In John 3:1-17,
however, Jesus speaks of a new birth and thereby suggests
something more like a transformation from within than a mere
change of direction.

Conversion is in fact a change of such magnitude that it can
be compared ultimately only with a *new birth*. This new birth
is the work of God himself who implants the seed of a new,

divine life within us through his Word and his Spirit (Jn. 3:5; 1 Pet. 1:23). This takes place when we believe in Jesus Christ (Jn. 1:12f.; 1 Jn. 5:1) who died to bring us life (Jn. 3:14f.). But this new life is that of the children of God (Jn. 1:12f.), and it differs from life outside God's family in that it is characterized by hope (1 Pet. 1:3), righteousness (1 Jn. 3:9) and love (1 Jn. 5:2).

Sometimes the way in which we become God's children is expressed by a different metaphor, that of *adoption* (Gal. 4:1–7). Although adoption may seem less drastic than a new birth, in both cases the reality indicated is the same. By nature we are not members of the family of God and have no rights within it. We cannot find our own way into this family, but only if the Father is willing to adopt us as his children. When he does this, we have exactly the same privileges as if we had been born into the family. Adoption is possible because Christ has redeemed us from sin and removed the blemishes that make us unfit to be called God's children. When we put our trust in Christ, we now become by adoption what Christ is by nature (Rom. 8:17). Paul puts this by saying that we receive the Spirit of God (Rom. 8:14), just as Jesus himself possessed the Spirit and was addressed by God as his Son (Lk. 3:22). The possession of the Spirit is the proof of our sonship. It is because we possess the Spirit that we are able to confess Jesus as our Lord (1 Cor. 12:3) and to address God as our Father (Rom. 8:15).

Many people, however, think that God can be described as the Father of all men. While there are one or two places which speak in a rather general sense of God as the Father of mankind in the sense that he is their Creator and Preserver, these passages are very few. The word 'Father' is never used in this sense in the Old Testament, and the only references in the New Testament (Eph. 3:14f.; Heb. 12:9; Jas. 1:7; *cf.* Acts. 17:28f.) scarcely permit the conclusion that God can be spoken of glibly as the Father of all men. On the contrary, God stands in the relationship of Father *only* to those who trust in him. In the New Testament era this means that he is the Father only of believers in Jesus. When the New Testament speaks of the fatherly care of God for men (Mt. 6:25–34), this teaching is addressed to *disciples*. They, for their part, must show the 'family likeness' by living lives of holiness and love (Lk. 6:36; 1 Pet. 1:15–17), and to this end God disciplines them so that they may become more holy (Heb. 12:5–11).

All this shows that men and women are not God's children by nature, and that each of us can enter his family only by the doorway of conversion and new birth. Even those brought up in a Christian environment must make their own personal response to Jesus. They cannot inherit the faith of their earthly parents, although there is no doubt that a Christian home can be one of the most effective influences leading to conversion. This is not, of course, to say that everybody must undergo a cataclysmic or sudden conversion. In many cases conversion may be more of a gradual process, and those fortunate to come to Christ in this way will want to echo the words of Dr G. Campbell Morgan, who dedicated his book *The Crises of the Christ* to his parents, 'Who forty years ago gave me to Christ, and who, never doubting the acceptance by him of their child, did from infancy, and through youth, train me as his, from whom I received my first knowledge of him, so that when the necessity came for my personal choosing, so did I recognize the claims of his love, that without revulsion, and hardly knowing when, I yielded to him my allegiance and my love'.

Union with Christ (John 15:1–11; Romans 6)

In the preceding two sections we have in effect been looking at the new relationship between the believer and God the Father. But there are also new relationships between the believer and both Jesus Christ and the Spirit of God. It is of course impossible to distinguish rigidly between these three relationships with the different Persons of the Trinity, since they all work together for our salvation. There are things said about Jesus which can be repeated in virtually the same words about the Spirit. Paul can speak in successive verses about the Spirit dwelling in Christians and Christ being in us (Rom. 8:9–11). It is, however, important to see what particular facts are stated about the relationship of the believer to Christ and to the Spirit respectively.

Although the Father is the source of all spiritual blessings, and everything in the new creation takes place in order that he may be glorified and praised (1 Cor. 15:28; Phil. 2:11; Rev. 4), the whole of Christian salvation rests on the work of Christ. This fact comes to expression in one of Paul's most characteristic phrases, found with slight variations in wording some 160 times in his letters. It is the phrase 'in Christ'. It used to be thought that this phrase expressed the nature of Christ as a kind of universal personality, to whom Christians have some sort of mystical relationship. Although this thought may sometimes be present, it is now recognized that the phrase has more of an instrumental or circumstantial nature. It expresses the fact which determines the life of the Christian, the fact of Jesus Christ, who was crucified, rose from the dead, lives in heaven and will come again in glory. The life of the Christian is determined at every point by his relationship to this Jesus Christ. It is through the work of Christ that new creation is possible. The person whose life is controlled by allegiance to Jesus is a new person (2 Cor. 5:17). It is through their common relation to Jesus that Christians of different races and social classes experience unity with one another (Gal. 3:28). It is because Christ, as Lord, determines their lives that Paul can order Christians to live on a new ethical level (Eph. 6:1; Phil. 4:2; Col. 3:20).

Other expressions show that the person who believes in Jesus is brought into a close personal relationship with him. He becomes a member of the body of Christ (1 Cor. 12:27) or a part of the true Vine which is Christ (Jn. 15:5). He 'puts on'

Christ, in the way in which one might put on a new garment (Gal. 3:27; Rom. 13:14). Jesus speaks of his being in the believer and the believer's being in him (Jn. 15:4–7), and this description of mutual indwelling expresses the closeness of a personal relationship which can hardly be put into words. In the same way, Paul speaks of Christ being in the believer (Rom. 8:10; Col. 1:27). He can say that in effect his own self has died and now Christ lives in him (Gal. 2:20).

A new union has thus been set up between Christ and the believer. This is made the basis of important teaching in Romans 6, where Paul shows how the believer shares the pattern of Christ's life. Jesus Christ died and rose again *for us*; there is also a sense in which we die and rise again *with him*. When Jesus died on the cross, he died on behalf of all men, so that one might say that it is as if all men died in his death (2 Cor. 5:14). His death can be described as a death to sin, or a death as far as the power of sin is concerned. When Jesus died, he passed out of the sphere in which sin can exercise dominion over men (although of course it had no dominion over him personally), since sin can exercise no claims over a dead man, and temptation can no longer entice the person who is dead to its attractions. Paul now goes on to teach that the Christian may be said to have died with Christ – a fact that he possibly saw illustrated in the symbolism of 'burial' in baptism by immersion. (This was certainly one of the ways in which baptism was carried out in the early church, although it was not the only way.) When this happens, the believer need no longer be under the power of sin (Rom. 6:3, 6, 7). His old selfish nature, which was the base of operations of sin, has been crucified with Christ, and he no longer needs to obey it.

Similarly, when Jesus rose from the dead, all believers rose with him (Rom. 6:4f.). By his resurrection he entered upon a new life, created and sustained by the power of God. Consequently, Christians who rise with him – a fact that also may be symbolized in the act of emerging from the water after baptism by immersion – enter upon a new life which has been given to them by the same God who raised Jesus from the dead. Now they are to employ that new life in the service of God (Rom. 6:4, 8–11).

This identification with Christ, as a result of which believers can be said to be dead to sin and alive to God, takes place at the moment of conversion when they are joined to Christ by faith. But Christian faith is not the act of moment; it is a continuing attitude. It is by such continuing faith that the Christian is able to reckon himself daily to be dead to sin and alive to God. In any case it is a fact of unhappy experience that so long as the Christian lives in this world he is still confronted by temptations which attract his old sinful nature. Paul therefore exhorts Christians to persist in faith and to trust in Christ who is able to communicate new life to them and thus empower them to overcome their sinful nature. The Christian life is a battle, but it is a battle in which victory is possible because the power of God is available to help the Christian to win fresh victories over the power of sin.

There has been much controversy as to whether the Christian can reach a stage of complete freedom from sin. If his old self has been crucified with Christ, surely this means that he need no longer succumb to temptation. John states that the person who has been born of God does not sin, and indeed cannot sin because he is God's child and has God's nature in him (1 Jn. 3:6, 9). Some writers, therefore, speak of 'sinless perfection', and some would hold that by going through an experience of deeper faith at some point subsequent to conversion the believer may attain this 'second blessing' of sinlessness. Other theologians point out that the phrase 'sinless perfection' is not found in the New Testament, and that there is certainly no indication of any necessary second crisis as the gateway to fuller Christian experience. They point further to the clear statement that if we say that we have no sin we deceive ourselves (1 Jn. 1:8).

97

A correct interpretation of Scripture must take account of both the sets of statements stressed by these two groups. It is the case that John states that *all* children of God cannot sin – sinlessness is not meant to be the privilege of a special group – and also that we cannot claim to be free from sin. It is also true that he speaks of God's love being perfected in us (1 Jn. 4:12). John appears to be stressing the ideal which should be true of all believers – namely that they should be fully controlled by the love of God and therefore should not practise sin – and yet he is aware that we can easily deceive ourselves into thinking that we are sinless. No man, therefore, can claim to be sinless, and yet the ideal of sinlessness is held before him as something that is possible as a result of his faith in the power of God. We dare not set the expected goal any lower than God has placed it, and yet equally we dare not claim for ourselves that we have already arrived and that there is no room for further progress in sanctification. It is the paradox of sanctification that those who appear to other Christians to be most Christlike are most conscious of their own shortcomings.

However much theologians may disagree over the question of Christian perfection in this life, they all agree that the effect of seeing Christ when we enter the presence of God will be to make us entirely like him (1 Jn. 3:2), and this is a powerful incentive to be holy here in this life (1 Jn. 3:3). Such devotion to Christ may well lead to suffering, but the believer has the sure hope that he who suffers with Christ will also reign with him (2 Tim. 2:11–13). As one who has been crucified with Christ, he lives by faith in Christ (Gal. 2:20), in the certainty that one day he will share fully in the resurrection glory of Christ which he has already begun to know in part (2 Cor. 4:10–14).

Possession of the Spirit (Romans 8:1–27)

Our fourth way of looking at the Christian life is in terms of the gift of the Spirit to the believer. It is through the work of the

Spirit in our hearts that we are born again and adopted into the family of God. It is the same Spirit who conveys the blessing of union with Christ to us, so that it does not greatly matter whether we speak of Christ or of the Spirit indwelling our hearts (Rom. 8:9–11). He is the one who applies salvation to us and fills us with the power and blessing of God.

The Bible describes the Spirit most frequently as the *Holy* Spirit, and this adjective expresses what is the most important aspect of his work. It is by the presence of the Spirit in his heart that the Christian becomes holy (2 Thes. 2:13). He conveys to the Christian the loving and righteous character of God. The special name given to those who possess the Spirit of *holiness* (Rom. 1:4) is *saints*; the two words italicized are translations of words derived from the same Greek root. This title for Christians primarily designates them as those who have been consecrated to God's service and belong to him. No matter how unworthy and even sinful they may be, all Christians bear the name of saints. Note, for example, the use of this title in 1 Corinthians 1:2, in a letter addressed to a church which was far from being perfect in holiness. But those who are *called* 'holy' are expected to *be* holy, in the sense that they share the character of the God to whom they belong. Saints have to live in a manner worthy of God, and this is possible through the sanctifying influence of the Spirit. It should go without saying that the special use of the term 'saint' to refer to a dead Christian of especial merit (Saint Peter, Saint Nicholas, Saint Ignatius) has no basis in Scripture, and indeed the whole theology of canonizing worthy men as saints and venerating them runs counter to New Testament teaching.

The effect of the presence of the Spirit in the Christian's life is that he can respond with obedience to the moral commands inherent in the gospel. He is no longer to live according to the old principle of sin (referred to by Paul as 'the flesh'), but according to the new principle of the Spirit, which empowers him to fulfil God's law of love (Rom. 8:1–4). Since he possesses the Spirit, he is to submit to the guidance of the Spirit, to put to death his sinful nature and to allow the fruit of Christian character to grow in him. In Galatians 5:16–26 Paul compares in detail the results of living the old way and of living by the Spirit: the latter way leads to the 'fruit' of a mature Christian character, which is seen in a whole list of qualities including love, joy and self-control. It is important to notice that these are very largely social qualities, displayed in personal relationships. Christian holiness is very much concerned with the life of the believer in society, and is not merely a matter of his personal devotion to God.

Such a life of increasing holiness is one of the surest signs that we are Christians. The Spirit who takes possession of a person when he becomes a Christian (Rom. 8:15) and who continually strengthens him to live the Christian life (Eph. 3:16; 2 Tim. 1:7) communicates to our hearts the assurance that we truly belong to God and can call him Father (Rom. 8:14–16). Through his work we are being prepared for the day when we shall stand before God in perfect holiness (1 Thes. 5:23). Thus the possession of the Spirit is both the mark or seal of God's ownership stamped upon us and also the first taste of the full blessing which will be ours in the future kingdom of God (2 Cor. 1:22; 5:5; Eph. 1:13f.).

Possession of the Spirit is thus the basis of our assurance that we are Christians. Indeed it is possession of the Spirit which is the mark of the Christian. 'Any one who does not have the Spirit of Christ does not belong to him' (Rom. 8:9). A question which has caused some debate among Christians is whether we can draw a distinction between this initial gift of the Spirit, without which a person is not a Christian, and a later reception of the Spirit in a newer or fuller manner. Some writers refer to this later experience as the 'baptism' of the Spirit. We must be careful here to distinguish between the name of any such experience and the possibility of it. It needs to be said quite emphatically that when the New Testament writers talk about being baptized with the Spirit, the reference is always to the initial act of conversion and regeneration (Mt. 3:11; *cf.* Jn. 1:33; Acts 1:5; 11:16. The persons who were baptized in Acts 19:1–7 and then received the Spirit had not previously received *Christian* baptism and were merely nominal disciples). Nevertheless, this initial experience of receiving the Spirit may well be followed by a subsequent experience or experiences of being filled by the Spirit (compare Acts 2:4 and 4:8; 9:17 and 13:9), and there may on occasion be something of a crisis experience associated with such acts, as for example when a believer who has been growing weak in his faith and obedience to Christ makes a fresh committal of himself to God, or when a believer enters upon some particular service for God which demands a fresh equipping with spiritual power.

The human response (Colossians 3:1–17)

We have devoted a major portion of this chapter to a consideration of the Christian life as the gift of salvation and new life bestowed upon us by God. It remains now to discuss the nature of the response which we must make to God and the way in which we receive the blessings of salvation.

The fundamental attitude of the Christian towards God is *faith*. From start to finish salvation is the free gift of God in his grace towards men. It follows that there is nothing, but nothing, that men can do to earn salvation or to make themselves worthy of receiving the gift. If that were possible, it would mean that the work of Jesus was incomplete and that he had died to no purpose (Gal. 2:21). It is perhaps impossible to over-emphasize this cardinal tenet of the gospel, lost in the medieval church, and rediscovered at the Reformation. This means that faith, which is the biblical word for the human response to God's grace, is simply the holding out of our hands to receive the divine gift. There is nothing to do except receive what God graciously offers us. Indeed, even the process of believing can be called a gift of God (Eph. 2:8), although this must not be misunderstood to mean that man has nothing to do in order to be saved. When it is made possible for him to believe by hearing the Word of God proclaimed in the power of the Spirit, he must respond by accepting the call of God (Rom. 10:9f.; 1 Thes. 2:13).

Faith is thus essentially an act of acceptance of what God offers to us. But this means that it must include an attitude of belief that the promises of God are true. A person who comes to God must believe that he exists and rewards those who seek him (Heb. 11:6). He must believe, in however elementary a manner, that Jesus is able to save him, before he can receive salvation, even if he feels that he must pray for a greater faith (Mk. 9:24). Thus faith may be defined as an act of trust in the unseen God, based on what he has revealed of himself in the Scriptures, which testify to his great act of salvation in Jesus Christ.

Two further elements enter into faith. Negatively, it is *repentance*, a turning away from sin and evil. A true faith in God is measured by a person's willingness to leave behind the sins and false gods which have filled his life, and to allow God to rule over him (*cf.* Lk. 19:8–10). The very demons, says James, believe in God and tremble, but that is not enough to save them (Jas. 2:19). To be a Christian involves realizing that our sin has hurt God, and being sorry that we have grieved him. There must be a readiness to give up sin and all that God hates. This, of course, is not a 'work' that we do in order to placate God. Our whole trouble is that we love sin and cannot free ourselves from it. It is only the power of the death of Jesus, in which we see the full horror of sin and divine judgment, together with the depth of divine love to sinners, that can awaken our hearts to hate sin and love God.

Positively, Christian faith is characterized by total *submission* to God in Christ. A Christian is a person who turned from idols to serve God (1 Thes. 1:9). He yields himself completely to God so that he may be made perfectly holy (Rom. 6:13, 16–23). For the Christian, Jesus is not simply a Saviour to be trusted but also a Lord to be obeyed. It is significant that the early Christian confession was not 'Jesus is Saviour', but 'Jesus is Lord' (Rom. 10:9). If God has called us to a full salvation, that salvation cannot be complete so long as any part of our life is not yielded to the Lordship of Christ.

It follows that both repentance and consecration to God cannot be regarded simply as once-for-all acts by which we become Christians, but as ever-new and continual acts of believers. We employ the word 'conversion' to signify the initial, decisive change by which a person becomes a Christian, but a Christian needs to undergo a process of 'continual conversion', involving daily repentance, faith and consecration.

So long as the Christian remains in this world he is exposed to temptation and the possibility of sin. It has become traditional to speak of an unholy 'trinity' of opponents arrayed against him: the world, the flesh and the devil. In the New Testament, the term 'world' is often used to signify not the created universe as such, but rather the whole environment of man which is organized in rebellion against God and continually tempts believers to disobey God and follow its attractions (Mk. 8:36; Jas. 1:27; 4:4; 1 Jn. 2:15). The believer finds that the world has an ally in his own nature, for he is a creature of 'flesh', a word which refers to the fact that as a human being he is weak and liable to sin (Rom. 7:18; 8:1–13; Gal. 5:19–21; 1 Jn. 2:16). 'Flesh' does not refer merely to the sensual aspects of human nature (our proneness to gluttony and sexual vice and the like), but to the whole of our human character with its capacity for selfish and immoral behaviour. Behind this process of temptation there stands the figure of the devil as the supreme tempter whose aim is to destroy our obedience to God and our spiritual life. Although the Christian has escaped from his power (Acts 26:18), the devil remains active in tempting and persecuting believers (1 Cor. 7:5; 2 Cor. 2:11; 1 Thes. 2:18). Yet despite all these opponents the Christian has the sure hope of victory. Through his faith in Jesus he has the power to overcome the world (1 Jn. 5:4). By the power of the Spirit who dwells in him he can overcome the desires of his sinful nature (Rom. 8:13; Gal. 5:16f.); and he trusts in the power of God to overcome the machinations of the devil and his attendant demons (Rom. 16: 20).

It follows that the Christian life is a perpetual fight against the forces of temptation and persecution (Eph. 6:10–17). This element of continual warfare is termed 'perseverance'. Like other aspects of faith it is not a human achievement but rests on the keeping power of God (1 Pet. 1:5). The Christian trusts in a God who keeps his people from falling (Jude 24) and a Shepherd who is concerned that none of his sheep should be lost (Jn. 10:27–29). Yet here again this must not be allowed to become an excuse for indifference or lack of effort on the part of the Christian. The New Testament warns in the most solemn terms against the possibility of falling away from the faith (Heb. 6:4–8; 10:26–31; 12:15–17). The promises of God are not a licence to sin with the assurance of divine forgiveness. They are comfort to the believer who is struggling against sin, and they assure him that a power mightier than his own will bear him up. The person who is not concerned to confirm his call and election (2 Pet. 1:11) merely demonstrates that he is not one of God's elect people.

Thus Christian faith is a lifelong attitude to God. It means grateful acceptance of all that God has done for us, and it is characterized by three basic elements – trust in God's promises, abandonment of all that God hates, and entire commitment to him.

Such faith expresses itself outwardly in prayer and good works. Through *prayer* we demonstrate our faith in God. We draw near to God and praise and adore him for all his goodness. We express our trust in him by making our petitions to him and believing that he will answer them according to what is best for us. We express our consecration by praying, 'Your will be done' (Mk. 14:36). Jesus himself taught his followers how to pray (Lk. 11:1-13; *cf*. Mt 6:5-15), and we offer our prayers in his name, *i.e.* on the basis of the fact that he is our Saviour and Intercessor with God. Through him we have bold confidence to approach the throne of a gracious God (Heb. 4:14-16), and God's Spirit himself assists us in our prayers (Rom. 8:26f.).

If faith is expressed towards God in prayer, it finds expression towards our fellow men in *good works*. The Christian has not been saved merely for his own benefit but in order that he may do good (Eph. 2:10). While it is true that we cannot atone for our sins by good works, nevertheless real faith finds expression in loving and kind actions, and faith which does not issue in good works is not faith at all (Jas. 2:26). Paul describes true faith as a faith that works by love (Gal. 5:6). Similarly, John says that the man who claims to love God but hates his brother is a liar (1 Jn. 4:20).

This shows us that faith and the Christian life are not simply a matter of individual relationship with God. Being a Christian affects our whole situation in the world and all our human relationships. In the next chapter we shall consider particularly the place of the Christian as a member of the new people of God in the church.

Questions for study and discussion

1. *What grounds has a Christian for being sure (a) that he is now a son of God, and (b) that he will enter into the life of heaven?*

2. *Martin Luther once described the state of a Christian being 'simul justus et peccator' (at the same time justified and yet a sinner): what does this description mean, and would you accept it?*

3. *Discuss whether holiness is primarily to be seen in the area of personal human relationships in the light of such a passage as Galatians 5:13-26.*

4. *Does the doctrine of the power of the Holy Spirit in the life of the Christian add anything that is not contained in the doctrine of the Christian's identification by faith with Christ in his death and resurrection?*

5. *What do you think is meant by the 'greater works' in John 14:12?*

7

The Christian community

'Sir, you wish to serve God and go to heaven? Remember that you cannot serve him alone. You must therefore find companions or make them; the Bible knows nothing of solitary religion.' These famous words of an unknown friend of John Wesley emphasize the vital fact that a person cannot be a Christian on his own, unless perhaps he is on a desert island with no Man Friday around. It is not, however, in the first instance, a matter of making companions, as if the Christian community were something we create. Rather, a person cannot become a Christian by faith in Jesus Christ, without at the same time becoming a member of the people of God along with all his fellow believers and sharing in the life of the church (1 Cor. 1:26). Indeed, we could not have come to know Jesus without the testimony of other Christians, their work in translating and distributing the Bible, and their prayers for us. Jesus came not to save individuals in isolation from one another, but to found a new community of people who would build one another up in the faith and evangelize the world. We must now explore what is meant by the church and what are its functions.

The nature of the church (Matthew 16:13–28)

If there was one phrase which Jesus used more than any other in his teaching it was the 'kingdom (or kingship) of God' (Mk. 1:14f.). By this phrase he meant both the sovereign, saving action of God, revealed in his own ministry, and the sphere where God's blessings are available, both now and in the next world. Clearly this phrase is a corporate one, showing that the purpose of God was the establishment of a people who would own God as king through Jesus Christ. This people is the church.

The church, of course, is not the same thing as the kingdom of God. The latter term primarily refers to the action of God, his kingship, while the former indicates a group of people. The problem of terminology is further complicated by the fact that the word 'church' is used in a variety of senses. Properly speaking, it means the people of God, but in modern usage it has come very often to refer to a human organization or to a building, and it is impossible to reverse this development in the use of the word. We can, however, gain some clarity by distinguishing between the 'visible' church, which consists of all the people who are outwardly members of it, and the 'invisible' church, which consists of all people who truly have faith in Jesus Christ (cf. 1 Jn. 2:19). It is the members of the 'invisible' church who have accepted the kingship of God and entered into the blessings of his rule. At the same time, the church is the means by which God extends his rule.

The establishment of the church was the climax of God's plan for mankind. The Old Testament tells the story of how God chose the nation of Israel so that they might be his people and he might be their God (1 Sa. 12:12). Sadly the story tells how Israel time and again refused to accept God as king (1 Sa. 8:7). When Jesus came, he brought God's last appeal to Israel, but by and large the people rejected him. So he turned to his small group of twelve disciples and announced that the blessings of God's kingship were for them and not for disobedient Israel. They were to be the nucleus of a new Israel, the church of God (Mt. 21:43; 16:18; Lk. 12:32). The church can thus be understood as the new Israel, composed of those who accept Jesus as the Messiah, and entry to it is by becoming a disciple of Jesus and owning him as Lord.

We can therefore speak of the church as having existed in the Old Testament (Acts 7:38), being composed of the Jewish people. Already at this stage it included those who were truly God's people and those who were so only outwardly and nominally. The church began anew in the company of Jesus' disciples. But its real beginning is to be seen on the Day of Pentecost. Only then was the kingdom of God manifested in power by the victory of Jesus on the cross and by the gift of the Holy Spirit to the disciples. Properly speaking, we should reserve the name of 'church' for the new people of God who came into being at Pentecost.

But it will already have become apparent that the New Testament church is continuous with the Old Testament people of God. The Jews are not excluded from the new people of God, provided that they believe in Jesus as the Messiah; but the church has replaced the race of the Jews as the Israel of God. This can be seen from the way in which the words used to describe the church have often a background in the Old Testament descriptions of the people of God. The word *church* itself (Gk. *ekklēsia*) is found in the Greek version of the Old Testament to mean the assembly of God's people. Christians are the *people* of God, and the significant thing is that this people includes both Jews and Gentiles who believe in Christ (Acts 15:14; Rom. 9:24–26; 2 Cor. 6:16; Tit. 2:14; 1 Pet. 2:9f.). They are called the *Israel* of God (Gal. 6:16; Eph. 2:12, 19). They are the *flock* of God, and he is their Shepherd (Lk. 12:32; Jn. 10:1–16, 26–29; Acts 20:28; 1 Pet. 5:3). They are the *bride* of Christ, just as the old Israel was the bride of Yahweh (2 Cor. 11:2; Eph. 5:22ff.).

The church can also be said to take over the functions of the temple in the Old Testament. The temple was the dwelling place of God (although, of course, his presence was not confined to it, 2 Ch. 6:2, 18–21). Just as individual Christians are now temples of the Holy Spirit (1 Cor. 6:19), so the church corporately is the *temple* or dwelling place of God (1 Cor. 3:16f.; Eph.

2: 19–22). It amounts to the same thing when the church is said to be a *building* in process of construction by God (1 Cor. 3:9; Eph. 2:19f.; 1 Pet. 2:5) or to be God's *household* (Gal. 6:10).

The New Testament, however, goes beyond the Old Testament revelation, when it describes the church as the *body* of Christ (Rom. 12:4f.; 1 Cor. 12:12ff.; Eph. 1:22f.; 4:4, 12, 15f.; 5:23). This phrase, especially loved by Paul, indicates that the church is composed of various individual members united to one another and to Christ as their Head in the closest possible manner, like the different parts of a human body. The power of Christ permeates the whole (like the sap running through the branches of the vine, Jn. 15:5), and the different members assist one another to perform their functions in a true spiritual unity. In this sense, the church can be described as having an organic unity, but it should be noted that the parts of the body in the metaphor correspond to the individual members of the church rather than to different local groups of Christians or even to whole denominations.

The life of the church (Acts 11:19–30)

If we accept the evidence of the book of Acts, the most characteristic function of the church is *witness and mission*. As Jesus was sent by his Father to bring salvation to men, so he sent and still sends the church to bring the good news of salvation to the world (Jn. 17:18, 20). The word 'apostle' is connected with the verb 'to send' and is used of those who were sent out to continue and extend the work of Jesus (Lk. 9:1f.). In Acts the Twelve are regarded as being especially qualified to bear personal testimony to the resurrection of Jesus (Acts 1:21f.), but the task of witness is by no means confined to them. Even persons primarily appointed to look after domestic arrangements in the church figure as preachers and evangelists (Acts 6). The very structure of the book of Acts confirms that the church is essentially a body of people with a mission. It began with

Jerusalem, and moved out into Judaea and Samaria, and then spread to the ends of the earth. The gift of the Spirit to the church was to equip it with power and divine eloquence for evangelism, and to guide its members where and how to bear their witness (Rom. 15:18f.; 1 Thes. 1:5; 1 Cor. 2:4; 2 Cor. 6:6). The preaching of the gospel to the Gentiles is the offering which the church makes to God (Rom. 15:16). The church is called to perform the task of the Servant of Yahweh (Acts 13:47; cf. Is. 49:6). This may involve much sacrifice and suffering (Col. 1:24ff.; 2 Cor. 11:23-28; 12:10) as the church faces satanic opposition (2 Cor. 11:12-15; 1 Thes. 2:18; 1 Pet. 5:8; Rev. 12:17), but it is the necessary prelude to the coming of Christ in glory to reign (Mk. 13:10). It is, however, a task which is certain of success (Mt. 16:18), for by the power of God a people who fear him will be gathered out of every nation (Rom. 11:25-36; Rev. 5:9).

The effect of evangelism is the gathering together of the new people of God in the church. According to the brief summary of the life of the early church in Acts 2:42, the first Christians devoted themselves to the apostles' teaching and fellowship, to the breaking of bread and the prayers. There is some dispute whether these four elements represent four different activities carried on by the church at different times or constitute the four parts of an early church meeting. In any case, here we have four basic aspects of the life of the church. First comes the *teaching* of the apostles. This is clearly not evangelistic preaching, but rather the instruction of the members of the church in their faith and its practical consequences. When the church is said to be built on the foundation of the apostles and prophets (Eph. 2:20), the meaning is that its basis is apostolic teaching, originally verbal and later committed to written expression in Scripture. It is by this teaching that the church exists. The words of Jesus are its food (Jn. 6:63) and the apostolic teaching is the Spirit-inspired continuation and development of the teaching of Jesus. Consequently, in the later books of the New

Testament we find exhortation to Christians to hold fast to apostolic teaching (1 Tim. 4:6; 2 Tim. 1:13f.; 3:14–17). However much the church must seek the guidance of the Spirit to enable it to express the Word of God in a relevant and meaningful manner for each new situation, the fact is that the Word of God has been given to the church in the apostolic teaching, which is the faith 'once for all delivered to the saints' (Jude 3).

Second comes *fellowship* (1 Jn. 1:1–7). This word means the sharing of several people in a common possession, and it expresses the fundamental idea in the common life of Christians. The church is a company of people who have one Lord and who share together in one gift of salvation in Jesus Christ (Tit. 1:4; Jude 3). Although the members of the church may differ in age, sex, race, colour, wealth, social status and ability, they are joined together as one people (Gal. 3:28; 1 Cor. 12:13; Col. 3:11). They share in one Spirit (Eph. 4:3f.; Phil. 2:1), and they must exercise mutual generosity as regards their material possessions (Acts 2:44; 4:32; Gal. 6:6). As Christ's disciples they are called to share with him in suffering for the sake of the gospel (Phil. 3:10; Rev. 1:9), and are promised a share in his glory and kingly rule (2 Tim. 2:12). In this way God, Christ and all Christians are brought together into an intimate union through the Spirit (1 Cor. 1:9; 2 Cor. 13:14; 1 Jn. 1:3–7).

The doctrine of fellowship has two important consequences. Those who share in the fellowship of the church must *love one another*. We have seen earlier that the characteristic of God's love is that it is not motivated by selfish gain, but loves to give freely without any partiality. Christians are to love one another in that spirit, since that is how Christ loves them (1 Jn. 4:7, 11; Eph. 5:2). Christian love is 'the greatest thing in the world' (1 Cor. 13). So the essence of Christian ethics is the command to love one another. It is summed up in the golden rule: 'Whatever you wish that men would do to you, do so to them' (Mt. 7:12). Such love is, of course, not confined to members of the Christian fellowship, but is to extend to all men (Lk. 10:25–37; Gal.

6:10) and to find expression in material concern and generosity (Jas. 2:15f.; 1 Jn. 3:17f.). It is this love which breaks down the barriers of race, sex and class. What is meant is that such love is not restricted by differences of this kind, and that it decisively alters the significance that may have come to be attached to them, although it does not necessarily remove them. Christian love treats men of all colours with equal generosity: it makes the colour of a person's skin a matter of indifference; but it cannot actually alter the physical colour of the skin, any more than it can make a male into a female. In the same way it can transform the master-servant relationship to such an extent as to show that it is wrong to treat another person as a slave, although it does not lead to a society in which nobody can be commanded to do anything.

The other consequence of fellowship is that the church ought to be a *unity*. The New Testament knows of only one church, since Christ cannot be shared out among competing and rival groups of Christians (1 Cor. 1:10, 13). All the members of one particular local church should therefore be at one in their allegiance to Christ. Nevertheless, the New Testament writers admit that not all persons who outwardly belong to the church have a true allegiance to Jesus; this fact becomes particularly evident when people cease to come to the church or publicly walk out of it (1 Jn. 2:19). There may be differences in belief between the members, and hence there may need to be divisions, so that the ones who are in the right may become apparent (1 Cor. 11:19). But this situation is not the ideal, and Christians should seek to agree in the truth and in their common faith in Jesus.

In the same way, since there is only one church (Eph. 4:4) which finds expression in local groups of believers, each of which can be called a church, it follows that such local churches should exist side by side in unity of belief and love. Church divisions should be geographical, rather than being based on differences of doctrine or practice. Our modern conception of denominations is quite foreign to the New Testament. From the point of view of John, the church to which he writes is the church, and those who went out of it to start their own rival group (1 Jn. 2:19) are not truly a church because they do not truly believe in Jesus and love their fellow-Christians (*cf.* 1 Jn. 3:23). In the modern situation we should probably want to deny that some groups which claim to be Christian churches are really churches because their beliefs are false – if, for example, they deny the divinity of Jesus and the doctrine of salvation by grace alone through faith alone. But we should not deny the name of church to groups which differ from us on some peripheral issue, such as the method of church government. Where such matters cannot be clearly settled by the evidence of Scripture we must respect the opinions of other Christians. From this it follows that all Christian churches should seek unity in belief and mutual love, while respecting the rights of each particular group to serve God and organize itself according to its own understanding of Scripture. It is clearly wrong to suggest that there should be uniformity of conduct of church services or methods of church government. The idea of one super-denomination which would embrace all existing denominations is one that is impossible to achieve, but the ideal of all Christian churches loving one another and attempting to come to a common understanding of the truth is basic and essential.

The third aspect of church life in Acts 2:42 is the *breaking of bread*, which is discussed below. The fourth element is *prayer*. Prayer has various aspects. In the New Testament we find the church and its members offering praise to God for all that he has done for them (Acts 2:47), seeking power and guidance (Acts 4:23–31; 13:1–3), and confessing sin and claiming forgiveness (Acts 8:24; Lk. 18:13f.). It lived by the promise of Jesus that if it asked anything in his name God would do it (Jn. 16:23f.). Such prayer might be offered to God in the form of hymns and songs (Col. 3:16).

We tend to group these last mentioned activities under the heading of *worship*. They constitute the service of God. The church has taken over the function of Israel as a kingdom of priests (Ex. 19:6), and its task is to offer spiritual sacrifices to God (1 Pet. 2:5, 9). This, of course, does not mean that the church makes a sin-offering to God; that has been done once and for all by Christ and cannot be repeated (Heb. 9:24–28). New Testament worship corresponds rather to the thank offerings and communion offerings which had their place in the Old Testament ritual.

Unfortunately, there has been a tendency to understand worship as what the church offers to God in terms of prayers and similar acts, and then to regard the main purpose of church 'services' as being the offering of worship of this kind to God. The result of this has been an impoverishment of the life of the church. First, it should be stressed that the actual term 'worship' is remarkably rare in the New Testament, and that correspondingly we hear very little of church meetings called together simply to offer worship to God. To be sure, worship is part of the church's service to God (Heb. 13:15; *cf.* Rev. 5:11–14; 7:9–12). But it is not the whole of it.

So, second, it must be insisted that the church's primary task is not to *worship* God, but to *serve* God, and this it does by carrying out the activities of witness and the building up of Christians in their faith. Paul served God in the gospel of his Son (Rom. 1:9) by preaching the gospel. Christians serve God by putting their lives at his disposal for whatever he may call them to do (Rom. 12:1). The performing of deeds of love is the kind of offering that pleases God (Heb. 13:16). In short, the church is called to serve God. Worship in the strict sense is part of that service, but by no means the whole.

Third, it follows that if we think of a meeting of the church as being essentially a means of worshipping God in the narrow sense we seriously curtail its intended function and give it a wrong shape. We do not come to church primarily to serve God by offering him our worship but *to let him serve us* by ministering his Word to us. The Son of man came not to be served but to serve (Mk. 10:45). When the church insists on serving the Son of man, rather than being served by him, it has got its priorities wrong. The purposes of meetings of Christians include the apostles' teaching *and* fellowship *and* the breaking of bread *and* prayers.

The means of grace (Acts 2:37–47)

God's Word and his gifts come to us in various ways which have come to be known as 'the means of grace'. In this section we shall consider the nature of these gifts, and in the following section we shall discuss the way in which these are mediated to us by human agencies.

Both as individuals and in company with our fellow Christians we receive salvation by *hearing the Word of God* (2 Tim. 3:14–17) and by the accompanying work of the Holy Spirit in making our hearts receptive to it (1 Thes. 1:5f.). There are two principal ways in which this happens – through the preaching of the gospel and through the sacraments.

It has been said that God had only one Son and he made him a preacher. In the early church the work of Jesus in *preaching* was carried on as one of its main activities. Right from the Day of Pentecost the apostles and their associates preached to unbelievers and taught believers. The content of their preaching was not simply human words, for through it the Word of God was conveyed to the hearers (1 Thes. 2:13). It possessed power to convert and save because the Holy Spirit was active in the proclamation. Those who preached it did not rely on eloquence, still less on deceitful means of persuasion, to get their message across (1 Cor. 2:1–5; 2 Cor. 2:17; 1 Thes. 2:5), but trusted in the power of God (2 Cor. 2:13–16) and were aided by the prayers of their fellow Christians (Eph. 6:18–20). Such preaching produced faith in the hearers (1 Cor. 2:4f.)

and acted like spiritual milk in nourishing Christians (1 Pet. 2:2). Although the New Testament usually refers to this activity as proclamation, it was of course not confined to 'sermons' and the spoken word; it included personal conversation and the use of letters and other types of literature. The modern use of visual and other aids to make the message clear and plain is thoroughly in harmony with the spirit of the New Testament.

Alongside the preaching of the Word, we have the *sacraments* of the Word, the visible means of proclaiming the grace of God. The word 'sacrament' is not found in the New Testament, but came into use quite early to describe the dramatic signs or acts which are means of grace for believers. Two such signs are recognized in Protestant churches: baptism and the Lord's Supper. The justification for linking them together is to be found in 1 Corinthians 10:1–14, where Paul points to fore-shadowings of them in the Old Testament; and also in the fact that both rest on the example and command of Jesus, who appointed them for universal observance in the church (Mt. 28:19; 1 Cor. 11:23–27). Ever since the Day of Pentecost they have been observed by Christians (Acts 2:41f.).

The sacraments are outward signs through which God makes known his love to us and we pledge ourselves to be his people. They are visible and audible presentations of the gospel. Just as we receive the grace of God through the preaching of the Word, so we also receive grace through the sacraments of the Word. But perhaps we should be more precise. Confusion has been caused by thinking of 'grace' as a kind of 'substance' given to us by God – as if along with the bread and wine of the supper God gives us a portion of 'grace'. But there is no such 'thing' as grace; to speak of 'grace' is to refer to the gracious action of God. The sacraments, therefore, should be understood as ways in which God tells us of his gracious disposition to us, and acts graciously towards us by cleansing us from our sins and giving us spiritual sustenance. Although, therefore, some Protestants are chary of saying that anything *happens* in the sacraments and insist that they are mere symbols of spiritual realities, it would be better to say that God speaks to us and tells us of his love both in the preached Word and in the sacraments, and that in the sacraments we are able to express outwardly the inward commitment of our hearts.

We cannot dispense with the sacraments, because they are commanded by God. He has provided them for our good, so that by the most simple means he may assure us of his saving purpose for us and we may indicate our acceptance of his grace. The sacraments are not the only 'means of grace', nor are they the indispensable means, but ordinarily God wills that all Christians should receive these pledges and tokens of his salvation.

Baptism in water was administered by John the Baptist to all who repented and sought forgiveness of their sins in preparation for the coming of the Messiah, Jesus. He prophesied that the coming Messiah would baptize with the Holy Spirit. The word baptism can thus refer to an outward act of cleansing with water or to the reception of the Holy Spirit. There is a third way in which the word is used. Jesus spoke of his death on the cross as a baptism (Lk. 12:50). Here he was using an Old Testament metaphor in which suffering and calamity are likened to the experience of sinking into water or being swallowed up by the sea (Ps. 69:1f., 14f.). This may suggest that because Jesus endured a 'baptism' of suffering, those who believe in him and submit to water baptism receive the benefits of his suffering for them.

Christian baptism, as distinct from John's baptism or Jesus' baptism of suffering, is a sign that we are cleansed from our sins and forgiven, because of what Christ has done for us (Eph. 5:26). It is also the outward sign corresponding to the inward reception of the Spirit, who also descended on Jesus at his baptism (Acts 2:38). It takes place 'in the name of Jesus Christ' (Acts 2:38), thus indicating that the baptized belong to Christ. They are united with Jesus, and hence they become sharers in his death and resurrection (Rom. 6:1–11). Finally, they are baptized 'into the body' (see 1 Cor. 12:13) and thus become members of the church. Baptism by water is, in short, the outward reception of the grace of God, through which a person is united by faith to Jesus Christ as his Saviour and becomes a member of God's people. Naturally the reception of salvation is not tied to the moment of baptism, but rather water baptism and Spirit baptism form two parts of one single act of Christian initiation.

Three methods of baptism have been practised in the Christian church: total immersion in water, affusion, *i.e.* the pouring of water over a person standing in a pool, and sprinkling, which is a development from affusion. Immersion aptly symbolizes death and resurrection with Jesus. Affusion, however, equally aptly symbolizes the pouring out of the Spirit, and it is impossible to see how the idea of baptism with the Spirit could ever have arisen if the practice of affusion was not used. It is in fact most probable that both methods of baptism, immersion and affusion, were practised side by side in the church in New Testament times, and it is not possible to affirm on scriptural grounds that either one or the other is the only 'proper' mode of baptism.

Baptism is at one and the same time a symbol of God's grace and of our response. The 'conditions' for baptism are thus the hearing of the Word of God, repentance from sin, and faith in Jesus Christ (Acts 2:38; 18:8). These are not 'conditions' in the sense that they represent a standard that we must attain in order to be fit for baptism. Rather, they are the characteristics of a faith which, in response to God's call, joyfully accepts the gospel, believes in Christ and publicly confesses its allegiance.

The practice of baptizing infants (as distinct from believing children) grew up very early in the church. The analogies of the covenant (*cf.* Acts 2:39) and circumcision (Col. 2:11f.) in the Old Testament, the strong sense of family kinship in the New Testament, by which the members of a household joined its head in becoming Christians (Acts 16:15, 34; 18:8), and the place allotted by Jesus to children (Luke has 'infants') in the kingdom of God (Lk. 18:15–17), have all combined to suggest to many Christians that the baptism of infants is in line with New Testament teaching, even if it is not explicitly taught. In such cases the act of baptism clearly cannot have its usual significance, since the 'conditions' have not been fulfilled and the infant cannot be said to have been converted. It still has to make its own response to the gospel. It can, therefore, be argued that the parents' desire to dedicate their child to God and to pray for its salvation might be better expressed in a service of thanksgiving and prayer (although admittedly this is not clearly attested in Scripture; see, however, Lk. 2:22–24), so that the child may experience personally the full significance of baptism when he has come to conscious faith in Jesus. On the other hand, however, it can be claimed that infant baptism expresses the fact that salvation is available for those so baptized and the prayerful confidence of the parents that their child will grow up to complete its baptism by conscious faith in Christ.

Baptism is the once-for-all symbol of our conversion and entry upon the Christian life by the grace of God. The *Lord's Supper* (or Breaking of bread) is the sign of the Lord's continual grace to us, the 'bread for pilgrims'. When Jesus gathered with his disciples for their last meal together, he took a loaf of bread, gave thanks, broke it into pieces and distributed it to them with the words, 'This is my body which is given for you. Do this in remembrance of me'. As the meal progressed, he took a cup of red wine, gave thanks for it, and as he passed it round, said, 'This cup which is poured out for you is the new covenant in my blood' (Lk. 22:19f.; the wording differs slightly in the other Gospels and in 1 Cor. 11:23–25). This simple rite was observed by his disciples, at first as part of a communal church meal, Sunday by Sunday.

What did it mean? Before Jesus died, when he inaugurated the feast, it was an acted prophecy that his body was about to be broken and his blood to be shed, in order that God's new covenant with the new Israel might be ratified. By giving the bread and wine to his disciples, Jesus was inviting them to share in the blessings of the new covenant. For us, now that Christ has in fact died and risen from the dead, the Lord's Supper means five things.

First, it reminds us of his death and its meaning for us. We do this in remembrance of him, so that as we receive the bread and wine we may remember that he died for our salvation (1 Cor. 11:25).

Second, as we give thanks to God for the bread and wine (which are in themselves tokens of God's daily provision for our bodily needs), so we thank him for the gift of salvation which they represent. This element of thanksgiving (Greek *eucharistia*) is expressed by the use of the term 'Eucharist' as a name for the Supper.

Third, the Bible often speaks of the life to come as a banquet (Lk. 22:29f.). The Supper is a foretaste of that banquet, for at it we show forth the Lord's death until he comes and faith is replaced by sight. Thus the Supper is a prophetic anticipation of the time of full salvation.

Fourth, Christians who look forward to communion with Christ at his heavenly table can have fellowship with him here and now. He is present as host to give us spiritual blessings which are signified by the bread and wine (*cf.* Mt. 18:20). The cup is a sharing in his blood, and the bread is a sharing in his body (1 Cor. 10:16), so that the Supper is a visible sign of the way in which we who believe in Christ are spiritually nourished by him (Jn. 6:51–58).

Fifth, the one loaf which is shared at the Supper is a symbol of the unity of God's people with one another as members of the one body (1 Cor. 10:17). At the Supper where they worship and adore the one Lord Jesus Christ and receive his grace, Christians are united in fellowship as the one people of God.

The ministry of the church (Ephesians 4:1–16)

No human society ever made any headway without the appointment of certain of its members to do various tasks on behalf of the other members and to administer law and order. Thus even from a purely human view we can see the wisdom of the church's appointing various persons to carry on its work. But the task of ministry in the church is not simply a matter of human convenience. God has appointed that there should be a ministry in the church. Jesus himself came to be a servant (Mk. 10:45; the word used here is also translated as 'minister' elsewhere). He is the pattern for the various other servants whom God appoints in his church. The ministry of the church is thus appointed by God (1 Cor. 12:28; Eph. 4:11) in order that the church may grow to maturity (Eph. 4:12f.).

In many churches today an accident of terminology has led to a restriction in the scope of ministry. The word 'minister' (*i.e.* servant) is used in the New Testament either for *any person* who has a task to perform in the church (Eph. 3:7; 6:21) or for the group of persons who, along with the bishops (or overseers), had a specific function in the local church (Phil. 1:1; 1 Tim. 3: 8–13). In the latter case the translation 'deacon' has become standard. Today, however, we often restrict the term 'minister' to *one* person in the local church, who is expected to fulfil a variety of different tasks of ministry, with the result that we are tempted to think that all the ministry in the church should rest on his shoulders. This produces a situation rather like that of a factory with a hundred directors and one workman: the output is minimal. We need to recover the New Testament emphasis on the ministry of a much larger group of people. Indeed it might not be a bad thing if we stopped talking about '*the* minister' and even better if we abandoned dressing him up in fancy clothes and calling him 'Rev.' – practices which are certainly not commanded in the New Testament and which are perhaps contrary to its spirit (Mt. 23:8–12).

A false view of ministry has sometimes arisen from confusion between ministry and priesthood. As we have already seen, the church is a kingdom of priests, and every member of it can be regarded as a priest (Rev. 1:6). This means that every Christian has the right to approach God and the duty to offer himself as a sacrifice to the service of God. He has no need of any specially appointed human priest to act as his mediator before God, since Jesus Christ alone is the Mediator (Heb. 10:21). Each Christian has the right to approach God on behalf of his fellow men in prayer (Jas. 5:16). All Christians are thus priests, and a person specially called to a task of ministry is no more and no less a priest than his fellow believers. Although the English word 'priest' is in fact derived from the Greek 'presbyter' (or elder), the word has so much taken on the meaning of one who offers sacrifice that it is misleading to use it of a minister.

If all Christians are priests, they may also all be regarded as having some task of ministry to perform in the church for its benefit as a whole (1 Thes. 5:11; Heb. 10:24). It is in this context that we should direct our attention to what Paul teaches about the gifts of the Spirit (1 Cor. 12; 14), since it is clear that these gifts are primarily intended for the benefit of the church as a whole, although of course they may also profit the person who possesses them. He teaches that there is a variety of gifts which include miraculous powers of prophecy, healing and speaking in tongues, as well as the apparently more ordinary gifts of uttering wisdom and knowledge and even of performing acts of Christian service and generosity (*cf.* Rom. 12:6–8). These gifts are allotted by the Spirit according to his own purpose (1 Cor. 12:11). There is, therefore, no reason to suppose that any particular gift should be regarded as *the* mark of the Spirit-filled believer, although all Christians should strive to be such people that the Spirit can work through them for the highest good of the church (1 Cor. 12:31).

There is some debate whether certain of these gifts (such as prophecy and speaking in tongues) were manifested only during the early days of the church or were intended to be perpetual. It can be argued that such gifts as prophecy were necessary before the church had the guidance of the full canon of Scripture but are less necessary nowadays. Whatever be our conclusion on this matter, all Christians should welcome whatever gifts the Spirit chooses to give to the church today.

Since the Spirit gives different gifts to different people, it is inevitable that God calls those who possess the appropriate gifts to perform special ministries within the church (1 Cor. 12:4-11). Such persons act because God has called them to be his servants and not because they themselves choose to do so. Their service is to be inspired by the desire to serve and glorify God and not for reasons of personal gain. Yet while they should seek no honour for themselves, they are to receive the respect due to their position as servants of God (1 Thes. 5:12f.).

A variety of ministers and ministerial tasks is mentioned in the New Testament, and no one precise pattern is laid down for the church to follow in each and every place. Clearly the Spirit guided the church according to its local needs. Since there is no pattern laid down in detail, our task today is to follow the basic principles which are apparent in the various types of church order found in the New Testament. In practice this means that there may be as much difference in detail from church to church as there was in the New Testament churches. The unity of the church does not depend on all local churches adopting the same pattern of ministry, still less on all being bound into one organization.

The most important task of ministry in the church is the *preaching of the Word of God* (2 Tim. 4:1-5). This includes the preaching of the gospel to unbelievers by evangelists and the instruction of Christians by teachers. One should perhaps include here also the administration of the sacraments of the Word (often performed by the same person, Acts 20:11), since for the sake of decency and order (1 Cor. 14:40) it is desirable that this be performed by those who are capable of doing so and have been authorized by the church.

A second task of ministry is *pastoral care and discipline*. The spiritual nurture of the members requires individual care and attention. Since the church is composed of persons who are still liable to sin, there will always be the danger of errors of faith and life among its members, and so there must be some form of discipline to maintain holiness and love. In the New Testament there is clear provision for the reproof of those who sin, even to the extent of excluding them from fellowship so long as they remain impenitent (Mt. 18:15-20; 1 Cor. 5:1-5). Such discipline is always remedial in purpose, and no effort is to be spared to restore the sinner to fellowship (2 Cor. 2:5-11). The sternness of the New Testament writers on this topic (2 Jn. 8-11) may come as a surprise to modern readers.

From its earliest days the church in Jerusalem felt a responsibility to look after its poorer members (Acts 2:44f.), and it was not long before people were appointed to care specially for this task of ministry (Acts 6:1-8). Paul also encouraged the churches which he founded to provide for the needs of the poor in Palestine (Rom. 15:27; 2 Cor. 8;9). Along with this work of charity the church also provided for the needs of those who had given up their ordinary sources of income in order to perform tasks of ministry (Phil. 4:10-20; 1 Cor. 9:14; 3 Jn. 5-8). The task of *caring for church property* did not arise in New Testament times, since at this point there does not appear to have been any. The problems of caring for property, however, are no different in principle from those of caring for funds. Obviously the church must delegate the responsibility for such care to appropriate representatives. On the basis of Acts 6:1-6 and Philippians 1:1, we can draw a rough distinction between persons appointed to the ministry of the Word and to the care of the church's material concerns.

In the New Testament at least certain types of minister were *ordained* or appointed to their tasks by a rite involving prayer and the laying on of hands by representatives of the church. This procedure was followed in the appointment of those who looked after the poor in Jerusalem (Acts 6:6), missionaries (Acts 13:1–3), elders in local churches (Acts 14:23) and evangelists like Timothy (1 Tim. 4:14; 2 Tim. 1:6). By this act the church recognized the divine call of such people (Acts 13:2), acknowledged their authority to act on its behalf, and claimed the help of God for those whom he called to act in this way.

One particular problem in the modern church is concerned with the *ordination of women*. More precisely it is concerned with the ordination of women as 'ministers' in the modern, restricted sense of the term to indicate those who have authority to preach and administer the sacraments. In the New Testament women carried out various tasks of ministry (Acts 18:26; 21:9; Rom. 16:1; Phil. 4:3). At the same time, Paul forbade women to speak in church (1 Cor. 14:33–35), and said that they should keep silent, and not teach or have authority over men (1 Tim. 2:11f.). There is a tension here between practice and precept which needs to be resolved. Some modern Christians simply ignore the teaching of Scripture at this point and claim that there is no reason why women should not be ordained. Others, who accept the authority of Scripture, either feel that the tasks open to women in the church do not include teaching publicly, or argue that the Pauline prohibitions were meant for particular situations in the ancient world and may be differently interpreted and applied in the church today. It may well be that in the social situation of the Pauline churches it was necessary not to offend Jews and others who could not understand the new equality of men and women in Christ (Gal. 3:28) and therefore to restrain some women who were using their new-found freedom to join in worship in an irresponsible manner and so bringing the church into disrepute.

The New Testament says little about the *government* of the church. At the local level there were persons entrusted with leadership (1 Thes. 5:12f.), but how they were appointed we do not know. In the early stages of the church it is likely that leadership devolved upon the first converts or those of mature age and Christian experience (*cf.* the use of the term 'elder'). By the time of Paul's later Epistles certain churches had a number of bishops and elders and deacons, but their precise functions are not known. As regards the relationsh ps between churches, we are again very much in the dark. The apostles and evangelists who founded churches plainly had some authority over them. Churches might also meet together to discuss matters of common concern (Acts 15). Elements of independency ('congregationalism'), episcopacy and presbyterianism can all be found in the New Testament, but none of these modern systems can claim that it alone represents the biblical norm.

Questions for study and discussion

1. *'To those to whom [God] is a Father, the Church must be a mother' (J. Calvin) : is it possible to be a Christian without having the church for a mother?*

2. *Use a concordance to discover the New Testament references to 'fellowship', and list (a) the persons with whom a Christian shares in salvation, and (b) the things which Christians share together.*

3. *Study the lists of forms of ministry in 1 Corinthians 12:8–11, 28–30, and discuss what equivalents (if any) they have in the church today.*

4. *What significance does baptism have for (a) the person baptized, and (b) the witnessing congregation?*

5. *What form should Christian discipline take in the church today?*

8

The last things

One of the most used pieces of jargon in modern theology is the word 'eschatology'. Strictly understood, it means 'the doctrine of the last things', and it is in this sense that we understand it here. Eschatology is concerned with God's final intervention in history to bring the present evil world to an end and to inaugurate the new world. But this act of God is not confined to the future, for God began his new creation in the coming of Jesus and the establishment of the church. Prophecies relating to the last days were understood to be in course of fulfilment in the early days of the church (Acts 2:17). In order, therefore, to understand what is going to happen in the future, we need to recapitulate some of the biblical story so as to put the future into perspective.

The final manifestation of God's kingly rule
(Luke 1:68–79)

The prophets of Israel were men who were profoundly affected by the evil and injustice which they saw rampant everywhere in the world. They saw that even the people of Israel were sinners in the sight of God, and they interpreted the various disasters which overtook them as evidence of God's judgment upon his people. They were perplexed by the problem of the suffering of the innocent and the prosperity of the wicked. They longed for peace and security to be established in the world. In these problems and questionings they were sustained by their faith in Yahweh as the God of history, and they believed that one day he himself would intervene in history to set up his kingly rule among men and to establish truth, justice and love among men. They looked forward to a day when Jerusalem would be the centre of a peaceful world, in which the offspring of David would rule the nations and bring salvation to all men. In short, they believed that God would personally intervene in the last days to establish his rule (Is. 9:1-7; 11:1-9; Mi. 4:1-7).

In due time God sent his Son, Jesus the Messiah, to inaugurate his kingly rule among men. Jesus proclaimed that the kingly rule of God was beginning in a new way, and indeed there was plenty of evidence for those with the eyes to see it that in Jesus God was intervening in the life of the world. The coming of Jesus was attended by signs and wonders which caused people to say, 'God has visited his people' (Lk. 7:16), and after his death and resurrection the Holy Spirit was poured out upon the church (*cf.* Joel 2:28-32), thus continuing the action of God. Jesus called men to enter the kingdom of God, and his disciples proclaimed the same good news of salvation by faith in him.

The new era promised in the Old Testament had in fact arrived. It did not, however, mean that the old era came to an end. The gospel message was not universally received, and sin and death continued to hold sway. The present era, since the coming of Jesus, is a period of transition or overlap. The old age has been judged and is doomed to end, and the new era has already arrived for those who acknowledge its presence and power by faith. Christians thus live as members of the new era in the midst of the old era. God has mercifully provided this 'interval' before he makes a final end of the old era, so that all men may have the opportunity of hearing the gospel and becoming citizens of the new era (Mk. 13:10; 2 Pet. 3:9).

From all this it emerges that the 'last things' have already begun. God's promises concerning the End began to come to fulfilment in Jesus, and the powers of the future are already at work. The coming of Jesus is the proof that God will one day bring the old era to a full end, and it is on the basis of what God has already done that Christians look forward with confidence to the completion of his purpose.

God has begun his reign! That is the meaning of the first coming of Jesus. But we do not yet see all things in subjection to him (*cf*. Heb. 2:8). The Christian hope is that God who has begun to rule in Jesus Christ will one day rule openly over all men. The present interim period will come to an end. The era of evil will cease, and God will establish a new heaven and a new earth characterized by righteousness. He will judge all mankind and those who submit to his rule will become citizens of the new Jerusalem, the city of God, and reign with him for ever. All this will be accomplished through a second coming of Jesus as the Saviour and Judge of all mankind.

Such is the prospect, seen against the background of biblical prophecy and the preliminary fulfilment in Christ. Now we must fill in the details.

The second coming of Jesus (Luke 17:20–37)

The Christian hope is centred on the return of Jesus. What he began at his first coming can be completed only by his second coming. As Christian salvation finds its centre and source in him, so the Christian hope looks forward to him as the fulfilment of all its expectations. The one who came in humility must come again in glory and be openly vindicated before all the world. In one sense there is nothing more to be revealed. The first coming of Jesus brought the full and complete revelation of God and the once-for-all act of atonement for the sin of the world. Nothing more can be added to this final revelation of God. Hence the second coming of Jesus in one sense brings nothing new. It merely consummates what has already been begun. The Jesus who is to come is the one whom we already know as our Judge and Saviour.

Although the fact of Jesus' return is clearly and abundantly taught in the New Testament, the details of what is going to happen are far from clear, and nobody should attempt to be dogmatic about them. So stupendous an event as the winding up of human history can be described only in symbolical and metaphorical language, just as we can speak of creation or of the nature of God or of the incarnation only in symbolical language. The symbols are not meant to be taken literally: the description of a Figure with a sharp sword coming out of his mouth, for example, is clearly absurd if taken literally, but if taken to signify the powerful character of his utterances it makes good sense (Rev. 1:16). Taken for what they really are, namely symbols, they tell us the important principles which are involved in the future events. Unfortunately, Christians find it hard to resist the temptation to press the details into tidy schemes, and as a result there has been much unwarranted speculation about the second coming, and Christians have often come into sharp conflict when defending their rival interpretations of ambiguous evidence. It is better to admit our ignorance of the details and to concentrate our attention on the unambiguous centralities and their spiritual implications.

Jesus himself spoke clearly of his second coming as the Son of man to be the arbiter of human destiny (Mt. 25:31ff.; Mk. 8:38; 13:26; 14:62). He indicated that his coming would be preceded by various events – the rise of false saviours, the persecution of his people and the increase of human wickedness (Mk. 13:1–25; cf. 2 Thes. 2:3–12; 2 Tim. 3:12f.), but he said quite plainly that nobody can calculate the date of his coming (Lk. 17:20f.; Acts 1:7) and that only the Father knows when it will be (Mk. 13:32). In fact there has scarcely been any period when there have not been false saviours, persecution of the church and the growth of wickedness, and one might be tempted to say that the coming of Jesus could happen at any time. The early church certainly believed this, and urged its members to be ready for an event which might take them quite unawares.

Consequently, teaching about the second coming is generally accompanied by exhortations to believers to live a holy life in preparation for that day (Acts 3:19–21; Phil. 3:20f.; 4:5; Col. 3:4f.; 1 Thes. 1:9f.; 2 Tim. 4:1f.; Heb. 9:28; 1 Pet. 1:7; 1 Jn. 2:28; Rev. 1:7). Men must not sit and idly wait for the day, but live in a manner befitting servants awaiting the arrival of their master (*cf.* Lk. 12:35–48). This of course does not mean that Christians are serving an absent Lord and that their motive for doing good should be fear of his coming and catching them unawares. The picture in the parables of servants awaiting the return of their master must not be pressed too far. For we live continually in the presence of the Master and enjoy his fellowship daily. If Jesus is absent from our sight, he is nevertheless spiritually present with us, and we do nothing that would interrupt that fellowship.

Although the coming of Jesus cannot be calculated in advance, there is nevertheless fairly clear teaching that it will be preceded by the final effort of evil to overcome God. Paul speaks of a figure who tries to usurp the place of God (2 Thes. 2:3–12), an antichrist (although Paul does not use that word). John states that there are many antichrists already at work in the world (1 Jn. 2:18), but this does not exclude the coming of a final upsurge of evil against God. If we are to take seriously the descriptions in Revelation of a final conflict (Rev. 19:11–21; 20:7–10), these point in the same direction, although some scholars think that here John is simply portraying in particularly graphic and concrete terms the conflict which is always taking place between good and evil, God and Satan. It is wisest to admit that we do not know precisely what will happen. What we do know is that no matter how great the power of evil, it cannot finally overcome the power of God. Evil will certainly be defeated.

One passage in the New Testament describes a reign of Christ and his people for a thousand years (*i.e.* a millennium)

(Rev. 20:1–6). Its meaning has given rise to considerable debate, and three main views have been put forward, known as pre-, post- and a-millennialism. Pre-millennialism is the view that the second coming of Jesus precedes his reign with his people (including dead Christians who have been resurrected) on the earth for a period of a thousand years, after which will follow the general resurrection of the dead, the day of judgment and the life of heaven. This view is often associated with the belief that some of the Old Testament prophecies about the people of Israel will find fulfilment during this period. Post-millennialism is the view that the second coming follows the ultimate triumph of the gospel in the world, this period of triumph being the millennium. A-millennialism is the view that the description in Revelation 20 is symbolical and that it refers to the entire period of Christ's rule beginning with his ascension and exaltation.

Each of these views is stoutly defended by its adherents. The first is held by dispensationalists, the second was held by some of the Puritans and is maintained by their contemporary followers, and the third is held by some of the Reformed tradition in theology. Where equally scholarly interpreters of Scripture differ from one another, it is best not to be dogmatic. For what it is worth, the present writer thinks that the millennium is simply one of the many pictures used in Scripture to describe the life of heaven, and that it is wrong to press Revelation 20:1–6 too literally to refer to a distinct period between the second coming and the judgment. Some scholars think that it makes a lot of difference to our present Christian conduct and hope whether we accept one view or another. But to say this is surely to ignore the fact that on all views the central expectation is of the coming of Jesus, and, provided that he is at the centre of our Christian hope, the details are relatively unimportant.

The important thing, accordingly, is to recognize that the second coming is the coming of Jesus as Judge and Saviour. The New Testament speaks sometimes of God and sometimes of Christ as Judge (Rom. 14:10ff.; Phil. 2:10f.). This is because God acts in judgment through Christ to whom he has committed the authority to judge (Jn. 5:22; Acts 17:30f.). At his coming Christ will judge everybody according to his works and words (Mt. 12:36f.; Rom. 2:5-11; 2 Cor. 5:10). The fact that judgment is said to be on the basis of what we have done is not, of course, a denial of the principle of justification by faith, since the evidence of faith is the good works which it produces (Gal. 5:6), and only those who have put their faith in Christ can perform works acceptable to God (*cf.* Heb. 9:14). The judgment involves everybody, Christians and non-Christians alike. In the case of believers there will be reward or loss according to the way in which they have used the talents and opportunities entrusted to them (Mt. 25:14-30; 1 Cor. 3:12-15).

Christ's coming as Judge is also and supremely his coming as Saviour. His people will be set free from sin and corruption to become like him. They will no longer be harassed by temptation and they will be made perfectly holy (Phil. 3:21; 1 Thes. 3:13; 1 Jn. 3:2). They will take their seats at his table and reign with him for ever (Mt. 8:11; Lk. 22:30; Rev. 22:5).

The resurrection of the dead (1 Corinthians 15)

The second coming of Jesus is accompanied by the resurrection of dead believers to join him (1 Thes. 4:14-16). The state of the dead before the resurrection is presented in various ways in the Bible. In the Old Testament it appears to be the common fate of all the dead to be in Sheol or the grave. While there are some inklings of hope of resurrection (Dn. 12:2) or of transfer to the presence of God (Ps. 73:24), in general the Old Testament writers lacked the fuller revelation brought by Christ. If the parable of the rich man and Lazarus is to be taken literally (which is not certain), we may be entitled to deduce from it that a separation already exists between believers and unbelievers, the former being at peace and the latter in torment.

But we must be careful about pressing the details of this or any parable. We should not, for example, want to apply the picture of the ruler gloating over the execution of his enemies before his very eyes (Lk. 19:27) to God. We get a clearer picture from Paul who knows that after death he will be with Christ (Phil. 1:23) and speaks of those who sleep by Jesus (1 Thes. 4:14). The penitent thief was promised that he would go to paradise with Jesus (Lk. 23:43), and the martyr Stephen saw Jesus standing in heaven to receive him (Acts 7:55–59). All this suggests that death ushers a Christian into the presence of Christ. Nevertheless, there are indications that this is not a final or complete state. The fate of the unrighteous is not described at all. We have to be content to leave the whole matter in the hands of God.

At the second coming of Christ two events take place. On the one hand, those who died as believers in Christ are raised from the dead and join his triumphal entourage (1 Thes. 4:14–17; 1 Cor. 15:23, 51–57). On the other hand, those believers who are still alive at his coming are brought into his presence to meet him as he comes (1 Thes. 4:17). All who participate in this event, both the resurrected dead and the living, are transformed by the power of God and receive a new body. Since physical flesh and blood cannot inherit the kingdom of God and immortality, Christians receive a new 'spiritual' body (1 Cor. 15:44). Just as a seed 'dies' and gives place to a plant which is organically related to it but very different in appearance, so our present physical bodies will give place to new and perfect spiritual bodies fit for the life of heaven (Phil. 3:20f.). What this means is beyond our comprehension, since the concept of heaven itself is unimaginable, but we may perhaps draw an analogy from the transfigured and resurrected glorious body of Jesus (Mk. 9:2f.; Lk. 24:39). The significance of the point is that Christians do not look forward merely to the survival of an immaterial soul – with the consequence that the present physical body and its life are ultimately of no significance. There is a real continuity between our present physical bodily life and our future spiritual bodily life. Salvation is concerned with the whole person and not merely with a part of it. The life of heaven is to be a continuation on a more grand and glorious scale of life in Christ on earth.

Those who are not members of Christ's people naturally do not share in the glorification which characterizes the resurrection of Christians. There is, however, a resurrection of the unrighteous so that they may appear before God and Christ on the day of judgment (Mt. 25:41ff.; Jn. 5:28f.; Acts 24:15; Rev. 20:11–15). The judgment which has already been passed on them in this life is ratified (Jn. 3:18f.).

Those who are judged in this way are those who have refused the gospel of Jesus Christ and remained in their sins. They are not fit to enter into the heavenly presence of God and of Christ, and therefore they are excluded from the presence of God (2 Thes. 1:9). This fate is described as eternal punishment (2 Thes. 1:9) or as a lake of fire where there is eternal punishment (Rev. 20:10, 15). Opinions differ as to whether this means eternal conscious torment or annihilation. The question is again one of how far the biblical imagery used to describe the after-life is to be taken literally. Those who adopt the latter alternative stress that it in no way minimizes the severity of divine judgment on the wicked, annihilation being a fate sufficiently dreadful in itself. Nor does this view deny that the wicked do have to appear before God and bear his judgment. There is no suggestion that annihilation takes place at the same point as physical death.

A particular problem is raised by the fate of those who have never heard the gospel and had the opportunity of freely responding to it. The New Testament does not speculate much on this matter. It is much more concerned to place before the church its solemn responsibility to preach the gospel to all men, so that all may have the opportunity of enjoying the blessings of salvation in this life and in the hereafter. Nevertheless, there are hints that the heathen will be judged according to how they have responded to the light which they have had. There are some grounds for holding that men whose way of life was such that they would have accepted Christ if they had had the opportunity to do so will be saved at the last day, because the sacrifice of Christ avails for them also (Mt. 25:31ff.; Rom. 2:12–16). We can safely entrust them to the great mercy and utter justice of God who desires that all men should be saved and come to a knowledge of the truth (1 Tim. 2:4).

To affirm this is not the same thing as saying that all men will eventually be saved. Some people think that although the Bible contains numerous warnings about the possibility of the wicked being cast into hell, nobody will in fact finally be sent there: the mercy of God is such that he would not consign any person to hell, and the power of his love is such that all men must eventually respond to it, even if that response comes only after some kind of purgatorial suffering. The fact that Christ is said to have preached to the spirits in prison (1 Pet. 3:19f.; cf. 4:6) is sometimes adduced in support of this view, although this is not what the passage implies: it speaks rather of the proclamation of Christ's victory over all forces arrayed against him.

Two things must be said about this view. First, there is no suggestion in the New Testament of any kind of purgatorial suffering after the completion of which a person may reach heaven: such a suggestion would imply that salvation depends upon human acceptability to God rather than upon the finished work of Christ. A person's fate in the next life depends upon his response to Christ in this life (Lk. 12:8f.; 2 Cor. 6:1f.). Second, we must distinguish between the universal offer of God's mercy and universal acceptance of that offer. The universal availability of divine grace is clearly taught in the New Testament (Jn. 3:16). But universal acceptance of grace is not taught. Jesus clearly stated that not all will be able to enter the kingdom of God (Lk. 13:23f.). Nobody, therefore, can

137

presume on the mercy of God to save him despite a life of sin and impenitence, and the church cannot evade its evangelistic responsibility by claiming that God will save everybody in the end anyhow. The doctrine of universalism inevitably weakens the moral and spiritual responsibility of men and blunts the evangelistic and missionary fervour of the church. It has no support in Scripture and a false soft-heartedness should not blind us to what is taught there: the awful responsibility of accepting the gospel in this life.

The life of heaven (Revelation 21:1–22:5)

With the day of judgment comes the end of the present world system, corrupted as it is by sin and evil (Rom. 8:19–23). The old era comes to a final end, and it is replaced by a new era. A new heaven and a new earth come into being, and since they are righteous they are eternal (2 Pet. 3:13). The new home of redeemed men and women is spoken of as a new Jerusalem, for it is the holy city to which the earthly, sinful Jerusalem points. Sin and sorrow pass away, and eternal bliss is the lot of God's people. The old is finished and all things become new.

It is possible to concentrate attention on the various pictures used to describe the future life of believers – the great banquet, the heavenly city, the river of life with its fruit-bearing trees – and to miss the reality to which they all point: the life of heaven is heavenly life because it is life with God and Jesus. The fellowship between man and his Creator, which was broken by sin, is now fully restored. God's presence among his people is no longer confined to his temple, as in the imagery of the Old Testament (but see also Is. 57:15), or to his unseen presence among believers (Mt. 18:20); he is visibly in the midst of them, and they can see his face. Both the Father and the Son are the light of the new Jerusalem, and the Spirit of God summons men to enter the city (Rev. 22:17). Thus, finally, redeemed men and women enter into that fellowship of love which binds

Father, Son and Holy Spirit together, and the holy love of God becomes final and full and victorious reality (1 Cor. 13:13). God is at last all in all (1 Cor. 15:28).

Questions for study and discussion

1. *'If for this life only we have hoped in Christ, we are of all men most to be pitied'* (1 Cor. 15:19) : *discuss.*

2. *If Christians are merely 'strangers and pilgrims' in this world, how far should they participate in its life? Should they simply concentrate on preparing themselves and other people for the after-life? If not, why not?*

3. *Discuss whether the different forms of millennialism make any difference to the present Christian lives of those who hold them.*

4. *'In a universe of love there can be no heaven which tolerates a chamber of horrors, no hell for any which does not at the same time make it a hell for God'* (*J. A. T. Robinson*) : *how would you answer this criticism of the New Testament doctrine of the final destiny of the wicked?*

5. *If heaven is not rightly pictured in terms of figures dressed in nightgowns, sitting on clouds and playing harps, what sort of pictures can we use to express its true character?*

Further reading

This list is confined to books and booklets written at a fairly simple level; theological students will need to turn to more solid works. The books listed are all currently in print (except where marked o/p), and are published by Inter-Varsity Press, except where otherwise indicated.

GENERAL
Evangelical belief. An explanation of the doctrinal basis of the UCCF (1973).
T. C. Hammond, *In understanding be men.* Revised by D. F. Wright (1968).

CHAPTER 2
R. M. Horn, *The book that speaks for itself* (1969).
D. M. Lloyd-Jones, *Authority* (1958).
A. M. Stibbs, *Understanding God's Word.* Revised by D. and C. Wenham (1976).
J. W. Wenham, *Christ and the Bible* (1972).

CHAPTER 3
R. T. France, *The living God* (1970).
J. I. Packer, *Knowing God* (1973).

CHAPTER 4
H. Silvester, *Arguing with God* (1971).

J. W. Wenham, *The goodness of God* (1974).

CHAPTER 5
G. Bridger, *A day that changed the world* (1975).
R. T. France, *The man they crucified* (1975).
M. Green, *Man alive!* (1967).
I. H. Marshall, *The work of Christ* (Paternoster Press, 1969).
L. Morris, *The Lord from heaven* (1974).
J. R. W. Stott, *Basic Christianity* (1971).

CHAPTER 6
R. M. Horn, *Go free!* (1976).
L. Morris, *Spirit of the living God* (1972).
J. Philip, *Christian maturity* (1973).
K. Prior, *The way of holiness* (1972).
J. R. W. Stott, *Baptism and fullness* (1975).

CHAPTER 7
D. Bridge and D. Phypers, *Spiritual gifts and the church* (1973).
M. Goldsmith, *Don't just stand there . . . The why and how of mission today* (1976).
M. Griffiths, *Cinderella with amnesia. A practical discussion of the relevance of the church* (1975).
L. Morris, *Ministers of God* (o/p).
A. M. Stibbs, *God's church* (o/p).

CHAPTER 8
G. T. Manley, *The return of Christ* (o/p).
S. Travis, *The Jesus hope* (1974).

Index of Scripture passages for study

Subject index